W9-ANK-189

Imprisonment in America

**Michael Sherman and
Gordon Hawkins**

Imprisonment in America

Choosing the Future

*The University of Chicago Press
Chicago and London*

The University of Chicago Press, Chicago 60637
The University of Chicago Press, Ltd., London

© 1981 by The University of Chicago
All rights reserved. Published 1981

Printed in the United States of America
88 87 86 85 84 83 82 81   5 4 3 2 1

Library of Congress Cataloging in Publication Data

Sherman, Michael E.
  Imprisonment in America.

  (Studies in crime and justice)
  Includes bibliographical references and index.
  I. Imprisonment—United States. 2. Prisons—
United States. I. Hawkins, Gordon, 1919–
II. Title. III. Series.
HV9469.S53   365'.973   81-10453
ISBN 0-226-75279-8   AACR2

MICHAEL SHERMAN is director of Justice and Reg-
ulatory Studies at Hudson Institute, and a fellow of
the University of Chicago Law School's Center for
Studies in Criminal Justice. GORDON HAWKINS is
associate professor of criminology at the University
of Sydney Law School, and fellow of the Center
for Studies in Criminal Justice at the University
of Chicago Law School.

To Franklin E. Zimring

Contents

Preface

"Don't look back," Satchel Paige advised, "something might be gaining on you." Yet, of necessity, this book regards the future by looking over its shoulder at the past. In any consideration of the social institution of imprisonment—especially in any attempt to change it—the weight of history must be placed in the balance. The recent excellent works of David Rothman, Michel Foucault, and Michael Ignatieff have confirmed the importance of a historical perspective on any era's policy prescriptions.

This is, however, explicitly a policy book. In Chapter 5, the analysis of the past is allowed to inform some recommendations which mesh liberal and conservative views. Although in some cases we have been driven back to original sources, this is not a work of primary social history in which lessons are inferred from a mass of detail. Ours is an idiosyncratic view of the constraints imposed by traditions on future choices, and its policy lessons are not shared by many of the historians on whose work we have tried to build.

The genesis of the book may help to explain another of its features. In 1977–80, the first author participated in a major study (commissioned by the U.S. Department of Justice) of the American correctional system. The central task was to advise the Congress, through the agency, of the present and future needs of the country's prisons and jails. The legislators, it seems, believed initially that the long-term future of the system was something that could be forecasted or projected with confidence. On the surface, this may seem a sensible goal. Yet as some of the researchers argued at the time and as this book maintains, this is not the way to approach the problem. To convert a policy analysis into a mechanical forecasting exercise is not only impossible in any respectable professional way, it is potentially dangerous.

Some of the dangers are addressed below, and others are examined by Kenneth Carlson in the project's report, *American Prisons and Jails*. Here we simply note that a great deal of correctional policy is currently made by this misguided reliance on forecasting the demand of an inexorable prison population and meeting it with a supply of cells. In many jurisdictions, such efforts produce only the familiar cycle of building, renewed crowding, and more building. Our book is aimed at these policymakers. They do not have to let the future sweep over them; rather than predicting it, they must choose it.

Legislators are necessarily generalists, but implicitly they use images of the past and the future to guide their decisions. Without a more explicit and critical view of these images, they will almost certainly prescribe for the American prison in its third century the same problems that have plagued it in the previous two.

Acknowledgments

Our central debt, to Franklin Zimring, is reflected in the dedication. His personal energy and critical intelligence sustained us many times during a lull in the proceedings. Other blameless individuals include Norval Morris and James Jacobs, who commented on the whole manuscript; Lloyd Ohlin, who impressed upon us the proper scarcity of the resource of imprisonment; Andrew von Hirsch, who emphasized the dangers of the supply-demand analogy in the making of prison policy; and Kenneth Carlson, who tried to ensure that we did not violate his high standards for the use of numbers in policy-making.

Our institutional debts are also extended. The University of Chicago Law School's Center for Studies in Criminal Justice, the Hudson Institute, and the Center for Advanced Study in the Behavioral Sciences at Stanford provided varied but essential help. Abt Associates expertly collected and analyzed the data in Chapter 2. The National Institute of Justice supported earlier work by Michael Sherman, and Gordon Hawkins received a fellowship from the Chicago Bar Association Foundation to begin the work that led to this book.

Itinerant projects are especially dependent on administrative support. Helen Flint, Elizabeth Scheuerman, Ann Bushmiller, Susan Bogdanffy, Sylvia Karjala, Barrik Van Winkle, Sally Mendoza, and Susan Olsen, at the University of Chicago; Robert Lindee and Barbara Witt at Stanford University; and Roberta McPheeters, Yvonne Swinton, Dorothy Worfolk, and Maureen Pritchard at Hudson Institute all know too well what we mean.

1 A Crossroad in American Social Policy

Introduction

When Alexis de Tocqueville came to the United States in 1831, his hidden agenda may have been to write *Democracy in America*, but his formal mission was to study the penitentiary system. On both subjects he was struck by the country's confidence in what he called "seizing the future." Today, 150 years later, many Americans lack such confidence about shaping events, yet they cannot avoid important choices which have been forced upon them. This is particularly true of the institution of imprisonment, which stands in 1981 at a crossroad. Conventional wisdom holds that the prison is practically impossible to change; yet today, along with some massive problems, there are opportunities for progress and reform greater than at any other time in this century. We do not predict a revolution in this critical area of social policy. We do contend that an unusual chance for change exists and that the real question is whether the nation will recognize that chance and take it.

We contend also that the subject deserves, and perhaps demands, attention from many Americans who try to look the other way. There are more than half a million adults in prisons and jails today. Six million jail admissions for various periods are recorded during a single year. One million offenders are under the supervision of the probation and parole systems; they can be locked up at any time for violating the conditions of their release. Still another 75,000 youths are held in special juvenile facilities, and the annual total of juveniles detained for short periods may exceed one million.[1] These correctional populations, as they are politely called, are large for any society. They appear even larger in a society which places liberty at the center of its political values. They represent a fraction of the citizenry larger than that of any other Western nation. The policies which have created them deserve serious thought.

The difficulty of balancing liberty and order would arise even if the American practice of incarceration were generally acknowledged to be effective. But the suspicion is spreading that many of the millions

1

of man-years spent in confinement are not serving any useful function. The problem is even more serious if, as the critics charge, society is taking away a great deal of liberty without getting increased order in return.

Even if political sensibilities do not stimulate a concern, economic sensibilities should do so. In most jurisdictions, one new maximum security cell costs $30,000–$60,000; another $7,000–$10,000 per year is spent to maintain each inmate. In the past ten years, the United States has spent more than $40 billion on correctional services.[2] To provide facilities that meet the standards set recently by the United States Department of Justice, governments at all levels would have to spend an additional $10–$20 billion; for reasons detailed below, they may soon be forced to do so. Moreover, these figures represent only out-of-pocket costs; a major accounting firm has estimated the real cost of incarceration (including such factors as the lost labor of the inmate) at $50,000 per year over a ten-year sentence, and $80,000 per year over a twenty-year sentence.[3] At these prices, it would make sense for the citizen, if only in his capacity as taxpayer, to look closely at the policies he is supporting in such style.

Yet despite these costs, imprisonment traditionally receives less scrutiny than do other important areas of public policy. Usually it gets no public attention at all: the institution of incarceration simply grinds away, and the people who run it are left to their own lights. When it does get attention, the scrutiny usually takes one of two unsatisfactory forms. The first kind occurs when a legislative sub-committee, a special commission, or a reform group discovers the problem of corrections. Concern is usually prompted by a prison disturbance, or by someone noticing, as if for the first time, that conditions in many American prisons and jails are terrible. Whether formed by the Wickersham Commission of 1931,[4] or the Attica Commission of 1971,[5] the pattern is pretty much the same: a flurry of intense interest, followed by a long lag, followed by an official report, and, with minor exceptions, a return to business as usual.

The second type of interest is more general, although it is often stimulated by an election campaign or by the report of a sensational crime. Public scrutiny of the prison system takes the form of an ideological shouting match between liberals and conservatives. Both wings are strong on accusations and weak on solutions. Too many liberals talk about preventing crime with tomorrow's long-term social programs, without attending to the communities suffering from to-day's offenses. Too many conservatives talk about throwing the key away, without considering the costs in dollars or in civil rights. Although the balance between these forces shifts over time, the broad-brush ideological debate is seldom fruitful. In recent years it has resulted in, at most, legislation allowing for longer prison sentences. Many legislative sponsors seem either unaware of or cynically indifferent to the fact that, in practice, the criminal justice system usually nullifies such legislation. Despite a rash of ostensibly tough laws regarding sentencing, the actual time served in prison has not lengthened substantially even in those jurisdictions where politicians have made capital on their hard-nosed approaches.[6]

The evasions which pose as scrutiny are time-honored, and both forms are very much with us today. The ideological battle continues, although it is becoming one-sided as conservatives are outbid in their calls for severity by politicians who call themselves liberals. The fitful attention to prison problems is going through a manic phase, during which every event is regarded as a major crisis, and making it virtually impossible even for thoughtful officials to plan beyond their morning newspaper.

The Crisis Mentality

In August 1978, Strom Thurmond announced to the U.S. Senate that "overcrowded conditions in our prisons have become a national crisis."[7] In support of this claim, he cited among others a warning in *U.S. News and World Report* headlined "Crisis Builds in America's Crowded Prisons."[8] A month earlier, Senator Joseph Biden had introduced legislation providing historically unprecedented federal funds for state and local construction. He contended that "the legislation fills an urgent need that becomes more critical as each day passes."[9] In 1979 the U.S. Justice Department published a warning from the American Correctional Association that current prison conditions around the nation held "the seeds of future Atticas."[10] The same mood has pervaded state governments. When a recent corrections commissioner assumed office in New York, he declared that his state was "rapidly approaching a crisis,"[11] and in 1980 the *New York Times* reported that in New York prisons "a major disturbance could erupt at any time."[12] Even at the local level, the crisis became a fixture on administrators' calendars: 1978 witnessed the convening of the Second Annual National Assembly on the Jail Crisis. By 1981, the dominant view seemed summarized in a bill submitted to the Senate by Robert Dole of Kansas which proposed revenue bonds and a direct federal appropriation of $6.5 billion to meet "the critical shortfall in funding for criminal justice construction, a shortfall that grows worse with each passing day."[13]

As Frank Kermode has said, "To be in the midst of . . . a crisis is what we all want, for it makes us more interesting."[14] But the issue is larger than that. The words used in public discourse, and the ways they are used, do more than express what people think. Language can influence *how* people think. The words are signals, and it is important to see their messages. In several ways, the crisis signals have distorted the policy problem facing the nation.

The first drawback of the crisis mentality is that it has forced the policy debate out of balance. People have become hypnotized by the quantitative, physical aspects of the current situation: the numbers of prisoners, of cells, of square feet. While no discussion can ignore these matters, it must be remembered that correctional populations result from decisions based on qualitative, normative assumptions. The prison population rises not by some mysterious levitation but because society, through its agents, decides that certain people ought to be locked up. To see the prison crisis exclusively as a problem of crowding and conditions is positively dangerous. It addresses effects while ignoring causes. It forces the debate into an excessive concentration on meeting a demand for prison space, without examining the policies and assumptions that underlie that demand. Worse, it may aggravate the very problem it purports to solve, because (as we shall show) new supply may not only meet the old demand but may also create new demand.

The rhetoric of national crisis may also lead to some panicky decisions. Consider the theme that the situation "grows worse with each passing day." To an official who accepts this view, not only must something be done but it must be done now, before matters get out of control. But the issues here are complex; they require careful thought. Most politicians are unfamiliar with them, and "Don't just sit there" can be a risky prescription. We doubt that the haste made by the crisis mentality will offset the poorly conceived policies that are likely to follow.

Our next quarrel is with the "national" part of the national crisis label. Traditionally, responsibility for providing adequate correctional space has rested with the state and local governments, whose courts incarcerate over 94 percent of all inmates, and whose facilities house them. Only 6 percent of all prison and jail inmates are federal, and the role of the federal government has therefore been small. However, a national crisis deserves a national-level response. It is this feeling that has injected the prison issue into the U.S. Congress and led one U.S. attorney general to appoint a Task Force to seek a "comprehensive national policy."[15] But it is not obvious that such a policy is possible or desirable. We do not deny the need for sufficient capacity to house those offenders who belong in custody in safe, humane conditions. But the real problems that exist are bad enough, without injecting a note of false drama by generalizing them to the whole country. There is a real danger that the Congress may be caught up in its own rhetoric, and not only provide national solutions to problems which are not national but possibly spread certain problems to areas of the nation where they do not now exist. Proposals to base federal funds for state prison construction on general formulas might have just this effect.

A final, serious drawback of the crisis mentality is its undue emphasis on the short-term. A crisis is something that comes, is resolved one way or another (by medicine in the recovery or death of the patient), and is gone. Its use here has policy implications which go beyond semantics. It neglects the long-term consequences of decisions that are intended to solve a short-term crisis. It implies that, when today's pressure is relieved, we can all go back to business as usual because the crisis is over. Unfortunately, matters are not so simple.

The crisis mentality encourages officials to regard prison policy as a "one-shot" problem, divorced from the past and even from the future. They believe, or want to believe, that it can be solved with a decision today and then forgotten. In our view, policymakers must see contemporary decisions as part of a long-range pattern, carrying well back into the past and well ahead into the future. This view may make these decisions seem less dramatic, but in fact they become more crucial. The entire matter is placed in a different light; regarded not as a transitory crisis but as a deeply rooted problem, its true importance can be appreciated.

With one qualification, T. D. Allman has nicely summarized our view:

> We should stop bounding every few years from one inadequate metaphor for the situation we face to another . . . the energy crisis; the population crisis; the crisis of crime in the streets and the crisis created by the revolution of rising expectations. The crisis of the falling dominoes, and the missile gap crisis. The whole history of policy discourse over the past twenty years often has been no more than a pantomime in which vast amounts of money and officials, technology and newsprint have been marshalled to fight crises that, it eventually was discovered, weren't really crises at all. We have tended to confuse unstoppable evolutions with sudden breaks in the dike.[16]

Allman's critique of the crisis metaphor is apt, but to replace it with "unstoppable evolution" would be equally misleading. We have substituted "crossroad": a place where the country can decide to change direction, where some barriers to free choice are down. Three current trends have merged to knock down these barriers.

First, the most recent rediscovery that many prisons and jails are overcrowded and that conditions are often terrible has been made during a period of expansive activity by the federal courts. While the courts had been informed of these conditions at various times in the past, their response to suits against correctional systems had always been that "courts are without power to intervene in the administration of correctional institutions."[17] This came to be known as the hands-off doctrine. But riding the momentum of the civil rights litigation of the 1960s, the federal courts of the 1970s turned to the prisons and jails in force. The U.S. district courts found many federal, state, and local systems in violation of the due process, equal protection, cruel and unusual punishment, and other provisions of the U.S. Constitution. They ordered new housing arrangements, classification procedures, facility closings, population ceilings, and hundreds of other constraints on correctional administration. Some of these orders have been partially reversed by higher courts, and some have been affirmed but ignored by administrators. But others have not been ignored, and as a result the institution of American imprisonment will never be the same.[18] Although much remains uncertain about the future of this development, the director of the Federal Bureau of Prisons is surely correct that in its pure version "the hands-off doctrine is dead and buried."[19] The rediscovery of the realities of American corrections will not go away as easily as in the past. Judicial intervention is forcing a profoundly different set of relations among the branches and levels of American government. It forms the core of a new correctional federalism and acts as a lever on the system, a powerful instrument for change.

The second crucial development is that the familiar but sterile ideological battle about crime and punishment has been refocused into a searching debate over the fundamental purposes of incarceration. Does America, and should it, put people in prison in order to rehabilitate them and then reintegrate them into society? Or should incarceration be solely a punishment for misdeeds, as declared by California's new sentencing statute?[20] Or is prison merely a device to protect society by incapacitating the offender? Indeed, is incarceration intended for the offender at all, or is its principal purpose to deter others from committing similar crimes? To what extent should the jail serve a different set of purposes? Is it good public policy to use the jail as a catchall to punish minor criminals, to shelter or contain the homeless and the nuisances, as well as for its traditional purpose of detaining those awaiting trial or sentencing? In any particular case, what is incarceration for?

These questions, of course, are hardly new; they are part of a continuing tradition of jurisprudence and penal philosophy. But as Chapter 4 shows in detail, the contemporary debate has severely weakened the moral and intellectual underpinnings of American imprisonment. Fundamental doubts have been raised, especially about the effectiveness and legitimacy of rehabilitation as a justifying purpose of incarceration. The effect has been to deepen the discussion of construction policy and to give the familiar philosophical thorns a new practical sting. Before answering whether to build more prisons, more people want to ask, "Why?"

Either of these developments—in judicial intervention or the purposes debate—would have been important by itself. But their intersection in the mid-1970s with a third development completed the present opportunity to choose a better future. Throughout the 1960s, the size of the prison population of the United States was either stable or declining. Then, in 1972–73, that population began to rise sharply. In five years it increased by almost 50 percent,[21] and this gave much greater urgency to the other two issues. In many jurisdictions, corrections resembled a rush-hour highway: the system runs normally at or above its capacity, so any abnormal load creates unmanageable difficulties.

We stress that by itself the population increase of the mid-1970s could not have created the current chance for change. Prisons have been overcrowded at many, perhaps most, times and places in American history. But in addition to feeding the United States' fascination with record numbers, the large jumps in inmate totals reinforced and aggravated the trends described above. In some states population levels pressed against judicially imposed ceilings. In others, crowding caused further deterioration in prison conditions and made it even harder for federal judges to look away. In turn, this intensified the debate over the purposes of imprisonment: how, it was asked, could the purpose of rehabilitation be served in those worsening conditions?[22]

The legacy of the 1970s, then, is not a national crisis but a setting in which major change is at least possible. Discussion of "alternative futures" is no longer academic; real options exist; familiar patterns and expectations are not shattered but unsettled. Federal judges dictating to state administrators, state legislatures reconsidering the basic justifications for prison, federal authorities pressing standards of conditions on state and local officials, the Congress considering for the first time whether to pay the bill for state correctional construction—all these combined in an unprecedented way during the middle and later 1970s. With established routines disrupted, a struggle was inevitable for the direction of any ensuing change.

At this writing (early 1981), there remains a chance for the serious deliberation that is one explicit goal of Mr. Dole's bill. "It is not the Senator from Kansas' belief," he said in introducing the legislation, "that funds will be made available in the budget for the immediate,

full-scale implementation of this proposal. However, S. 186 is designed to serve as a catalyst for discussing between Members of
Congress and representatives from criminal justice agencies and
interested groups. It is imperative that this dialog begin as soon as
possible." The pressure for change remains high, because many
prisons remain badly overcrowded and the purposes debate is by no
means resolved. But, since 1978, the annual rate of increase in the
national inmate total has not matched earlier levels, and whatever
we may think of this indicator it inevitably affects the national legislature. Many things are bad, but in most places they are not getting
dramatically worse while solutions are being considered. Sensible
legislators should be able to abandon the crisis mentality and choose,
without panic, the future they really want. In that mood, we may
pause here and review the contemporary debate about what to do
next.

The Contemporary Construction Debate

The specialized debate over prison construction suffers from a
familiar distortion: the reappearance of ideology in plain clothes.
Experts are supposed to provide the public with reasoned analysis
rather than personal opinion; but many penologists' discussions are
more ideological and simplistic than the statements made in the general liberal-conservative debate. Two one-idea positions battle it out.
The first group of specialists argues that the answer is simple: build
more prisons. Otherwise an increasing number of dangerous criminals will go free, either because there literally is no room for them in
prison or because federal judges will not allow local judges to send
them there. The policy problem, in this view, is the underuse of
incarceration. The prison and jail populations are too small; more
offenders should be sent to prison, and more capacity must be built to
house all those who should be locked up.

A second group of specialists also finds the answer simple, but
exactly opposite: refuse to build any more prisons, and reduce prison
populations by finding other penalties for most of those now locked
up. Here the problem is seen as the overuse of incarceration. The
prison and jail populations are much too large; the country has too
much prison space already and certainly does not need any more.

There is a parallel here with an earlier era in American history. The
germinal years of American penology were dominated by the great
nineteenth-century conflict between the proponents of the rival Pennsylvania and Auburn systems of prison administration, architecture,
and discipline. From a twentieth-century perspective, this bitter
controversy—between the Quaker case for reflection in solitude and

the New England/Puritan arguments in favor of congregate work—may seem trivial. David Rothman is correct in saying that "as both schemes placed maximum emphasis on preventing the prisoners from communicating with anyone else, the point of dispute was whether convicts should work silently in large groups or individually within solitary cells."[23] But those who participated in the debate, not only in America but also in England, France, and Prussia, did not see themselves as concerned with a matter of little significance. Supporters of the Pennsylvania system believed that their form of organization was not only more effective in achieving reformation but also recognized the prisoner as a human being rather than a wage slave. Auburn supporters argued that their system was more natural, more humane, and more healthy as well as economically superior. Moreover, these competing theories had important practical consequences; as Rothman recognizes, the controversy exerted "a critical influence on legislators' resolves to erect penitentiaries and officials' decisions on how to administer them."[24] Nor was this influence merely transient. As W. David Lewis notes, the lasting power of these ideas was such that "methods that were increasingly outmoded continued to be imposed upon most adult convicts for the rest of the nineteenth century."[25]

Today's construction debate shares some superficial features with that early controversy. It is certainly bitter, and there is plenty of rhetoric. Consider William Nagel, director of the American Foundation's Institute of Corrections and a leader of the antibuilding school. Attacking the Federal Bureau of Prisons' "Long Range Master Plan" for the construction of new institutions, Nagel published a pamphlet entitled *An American Archipelago: The United States Bureau of Prisons*. The clear allusion was to *The Gulag Archipelago*, Solzhenitsyn's study of Soviet tyranny. Nagel accused the Bureau of Prisons of being "construction crazy" and "isolated and secretive." The bureau's plans, he said, "are deeper and darker secrets than ever were the Pentagon papers."[26]

The probuilding school is capable of its own extravagant language. John Conrad of the Academy for Contemporary Problems has said that to oppose prison construction "means entailing increased misery, violence, and murder." He writes of "the stomach-turning future" of the nation's prisons where "men and boys will be jammed together like rubbish in a compost pile."[27] But whatever one's view of these literary styles, behind the rhetoric there are real issues at stake: differences both about matters of fact and their interpretation, and also about expediency and morality and prudence in the use of scarce resources. A debate which seems to be about a straightforward practical matter, namely, the construction of prisons, appears on examination to be part of a much broader ideological debate. Profound and intractable questions that have troubled all organized societies—What is justice? What must be done with criminals?—lie just under the surface of this innocuous matter of capacity supply and prison population demand.

Of course the analogy with the Pennsylvania/Auburn controversy is not exact, and the ways in which the two debates differ are significant. The first half of the nineteenth century was a period of what Rupert Cross has called "penological optimism,"[28] whereas in our time penological skepticism or even penological pessimism dominates the thinking of scholars and administrators in the field of corrections. There was, between the supporters of the Pennsylvania and the Auburn systems, agreement that the penitentiary was an institution with a powerful potential for good. They believed in imprisonment. Today, the criticisms of prison range from "no more construction now" to "no more construction ever" to "tear down the ones you have." The current dispute may not be angrier than the earlier one for it would be difficult to surpass the degree of acrimony attained by the nineteenth-century penologists, but it touches more fundamental levels.

The recognition that construction is the tip of the policy iceberg is fairly recent. As late as 1967, prison construction was not mentioned at all in a comprehensive review of adult corrections by the President's Crime Commission. Acknowledging that the capacity of the juvenile system was "under severe strain," the commission expressed no general concern about the need for additional adult prison capacity. Forecasting the future demand for prison space, it said that "the population projection for the prison system shows the smallest aggregate increase of any of the correctional activities"[29] of incarceration, probation, parole, and community corrections. The 1967 commission did not take a position on the issue of prison construction; its forecast implied that, where the problem of prison crowding did exist, the difficulty would resolve itself.

The commission had grounds for its optimism. At the time of its research, many people felt that a long-term rise in the nation's inmate population had been reversed. Since national statistics were first compiled in 1926, the period just before and during World War II represented the only significant interruption in the trend of rising population. But in the early 1960s the prison population stabilized and began to drop; from 1961 to 1972 the total number of state inmates declined by 14 percent, from 210,000 to 180,000.[30] The mid-sixties Crime Commission was working, figuratively and literally, in the middle of this development.

By 1971, however, the decline in the national prison population had slowed. Perhaps anticipating what was to come, the American Friends' Service Committee published the first major attack on prison construction:

> As a reform "modern" prisons may relieve the harsher physical hardships of doing time, but the essential punitive element of prison—deprivation of liberty and free choice—remains. When pressures for reform lead to demands to relieve "overcrowding" by adding new cell or bed space, the result is inevitable: the coercive net of the justice system will be spread over a larger number of people, entrapping them for longer periods of time. If prisons are overcrowded, ways should be found to cut back the mass of criminal laws and the types of enforcement that send so many people to prison. The construction of new prisons is not compatible with our view of the proper role of criminal law in a democratic society.[31]

It is ironic that the Quakers, who virtually invented the penitentiary in the seventeenth century, reinvented it in the eighteenth, and championed it in the nineteenth, should have led the charge against it in the latter part of the twentieth century. Other liberal groups followed closely. In 1972 the National Council on Crime and Delinquency (NCCD) said that "no new detention or penal institution should be built before alternatives to incarceration are fully achieved."[32] A report of the American Assembly took a similar view,[33] and in 1973 the National Advisory Commission on Criminal Justice Standards and Goals recommended a ten-year moratorium on construction.[34]

In 1975 the antibuilders became formally organized. The Unitarian Universalist Service Committee, with the assistance of the NCCD, opened an office in Washington, D.C., and launched the National Moratorium on Prison Construction. The moratorium started immediately to organize committees and coalitions throughout the country.[35] In 1981 it remains the focus and catalyst of antibuilding views. Whatever one may think of its recommendations, it is testimony to the potential influence of a small number of activists dedicated to a principle. Win or lose, it has changed the American debate on imprisonment for years to come.

Opposition to the moratorium movement has been less organized and less vocal. This is to be expected, because defenders of the status quo feel little need to form campaign committees.[36] Although there have been no specific counterorganizations, broader groups such as the American Correctional Association have carried the antimoratorium case to the public. Since we cannot assume the general reader's familiarity with the arguments, and since legislators may in any case find a catalogue useful, we have provided a critical summary here. Specialists may wish to practice their speed-reading.

The Case against Construction

The Most Expensive Sanction

A major reason for opposition to more correctional construction is its economic cost. Some rough estimates have been presented above: $30,000–$60,000 to build a maximum security cell, $10–$20 billion to maintain today's prison and jail capacity at consensus standards of conditions. Although these numbers vary by state and region, there is no serious disagreement with the Senate Appropriations Committee's view that "the cost of construction and operating new prison facilities is enormous, and the use of imprisonment is the most expensive sanction which can be imposed on a criminal offender." But it is not clear what specific policies this implies. The committee argued that "because cost makes imprisonment a scarce resource, it is essential that imprisonment only be used where necessary to assure the protection of society or the administration of just punishment."[37] However, protection and justice are not self-defining. The argument based on cost is almost axiomatic in character; imprisonment is expensive and should be employed sparingly. While useful as a reminder, the purely economic argument does not take us very far.

The Leading Incarcerator

Despite the antibuilders' injunction, the United States does not use imprisonment sparingly, at least by comparison with other countries. Yet the antibuilders feel that this fact further strengthens their case. "No other country in the world," says Eugene Doleschal, director of the NCCD Information Center, "imprisons as great a proportion of the population as we do, and the length of sentence for an offender in the American criminal justice system is several times longer than that of his counterpart anywhere in the world."[38] The inference drawn by Doleschal is that there should be no further capital investment in prisons. To us it is not obvious how any prescription can be drawn directly from America's ranking on the international roster of imprisonment rates.

A Long-Term Legacy

A stronger argument relates to the long-lasting character of prison buildings. In *The New Red Barn* William Nagel says that "the endurance of these monolithic structures is surpassed only by the tenacity of the assumptions and attitudes on which they were founded."[39] For an opponent of construction, he understates his case; the buildings often outlast the ideas that gave rise to them. Bentham's essay on the Panopticon was published in 1791; while few today have much regard for his theories of architectural design, inmates at Stateville Penitentiary in Illinois are still housed in four circular cell houses based on Bentham's model.

Of course, the perdurability of prisons can cut either way in today's construction controversy. Norman Carlson, director of the U.S. Bureau of Prisons, tried to use this argument against the moratorium critics. Citing Leavenworth as an example, he spoke of "the sheer physical impossibility of converting this old penitentiary into a modern correctional institution";[40] and from this impossibility he drew support for the bureau's new construction program and for the replacement of outmoded institutions with new ones designed for humane incarceration.

The physical legacy of a prison, of course, appears differently to different generations. The old institutions were designed for "humane incarceration" in the light of the conditions of their time. But this very recognition that standards change and buildings do not—except occasionally and at great expense—is one of the moratorium's strongest weapons. They have induced caution and second thoughts into a process that was traditionally done by rote.

If the government cuts taxes this year, it can and probably will raise them next year; but if it builds prisons this year, the effects may be felt well into the twenty-first century. This is not a prediction about broad social policies but rather a recognition that the tradition of American corrections is to build very long-lasting facilities. In common speech, people refer to a decision as being set in concrete. In penal policy, the American way has been to make this literally true. Except for plantation facilities in the South or some low security facilities elsewhere around the country, a decision is cast in brick and mortar that will last for decades. In principle, of course, facilities could be closed, torn down, or turned to some other purpose; in practice, this rarely happens. The general pattern, true of most of the country for most of its history, has been that prisons and jails have a long life. In the absence of major and conscious change, this pattern is going to continue. If it does, a decision today to build new facilities may be thought of as based on a fifty-year plan. The plan's legacy might be even longer. Two-thirds of all the maximum security space in the country today is over fifty years old, and 30 percent—unbelievably—is over 100 years old. Governments would not presume to plan for comparable spans of time in any other social policy, and they do not do so consciously here. But the effect may be the same. Many prisoners in the year 2030 will be housed according to today's standard of what constitutes adequate, humane, constitutional conditions. Unlike an economic plan, a prison cannot be constantly updated; the nation will live for a long time with the construction decisions it makes today.

Parkinson for Prisons

A related argument is that not only do prisons last a long time but that additional prison capacity also generates an increased number of prisoners. This is reminiscent of Parkinson's Law, which holds that work expands to fill the time available for its completion.[41] Critics say that prison population expands to fill the available buildings. "To allocate funds for institutions," says the NCCD Policy Statement on Prison Construction, "will increase rather than decrease institution populations."[42] Milton Rector asks rhetorically, "Would not judges who were once reluctant to commit, because of the conditions of the old prisons, now send throngs of inmates to the sparkling new ones?"[43] Harold Confer, of the Friends' Committee on National Legislation, claims that "just as the availability of guns facilitates armed robbery, the construction of new prisons tends to strengthen policies of incarceration." He also sees political pressure: "The tax-payers are going to say . . . why have you spent so many million dollars in constructing new facilities if you do not really intend to use them."[44]

The weakness of the moratorium's position here stems from over-statement. The possibility that capacity may invite population is presented by the antibuilders as something approaching a law of nature. The situation is better compared with Aaron Wildavsky's account of American health care, in which he found the country is doing better and feeling worse; the easier it is to see a doctor, the more people find they are sick enough to need one.[45] Similarly, in *some* criminal justice systems, excess prison capacity probably does erode mechanisms that might otherwise have limited the prison population. Especially where federal judges refuse to tolerate traditionally high levels of crowding, new capacity may make the difference between a stable or increasing number of prisoners.

The moratorium has a strong argument here, and they only weaken it by claiming too much for it. In some states, the decision to build more prisons is a decision to incarcerate more people over the long lifetime of the buildings. Over fifty years or more, today's decisions will affect not only how inmates live but how many are locked up. If a crisis emphasis leads to seeing the problem as simply a short-term demand for more prison construction, in some places it risks the reappearance of the same problem years later at a higher level of incarceration. However, the risk is not equally distributed among states. There is no law of nature here; if there were, there would never be (or at least not for very long) unused prison space. In fact many jurisdictions have had—and some have today—an excess of capacity over population, although the Parkinsonian theory cannot account for this. The antibuilders damage their case by generalizing an argument that fits some states well and others not well at all.

Alternatives to Incarceration

Arguments about alternative sentences are used to bolster the economic case against imprisonment: "If new prisons are not built, new resources and talents can be made available to develop alternatives to prison."[46] And these alternatives are in turn defended as more humane, which is obvious, and more effective, which is not.

A typical claim is that of the Advisory Commission on Intergovernmental Relations: "Community-based treatment programs—including probation work release, youth service bureaus, halfway houses, parole and aftercare—can be more effective than institutional custody in rehabilitating most offenders and in facilitating their readjustment to society."[47] We shall discuss the competing purposes of imprisonment in the next chapter, but we note here that the prison's critics often concentrate exclusively on the goals of rehabilitation and reintegration. The prison's defenders emphasize other aims, especially incapacitation. Even if the moratorium proved its claim that alternatives cut recidivism more than prison does, that would not resolve the question of whether prison works. The argument about rehabilitation is only one dimension of the "effectiveness" debate.

In 1972, the NCCD used the notion of incapacitation as a weapon against construction. "Confinement," it said, "is necessary only for the offender who, if not confined, would be a serious danger to the public. For all others, who are not dangerous and who constitute the great majority of offenders, the sentence of choice should be one or another of the wide variety of noninstitutional dispositions." By its standard of dangerousness, the NCCD drew a position that "only a small percentage of offenders in penal institutions today"[48] really required incarceration. Indeed, "in any state no more than one hundred persons would have to be confined in a single maximum security institution, which, because of its small size, could be staffed for genuine treatment."[49] Since the national prison population would total about 5,000 under this strategy, it was an understatement to say that "on that basis we have vastly more institutional space than we need."[50] Recently, the NCCD abandoned efforts to specify a numerical limit on population size. But the example shows that from a tenuous definitional starting point it is easy to reach a construction policy that would require not bricks and mortar but merely dynamite.

Humanity and Fairness

Both sides in the construction debate naturally claim that their recommendations are humane and fair. Remarkably, they do not disagree that present conditions and practices often violate both standards. Indeed, one of the most eloquent denunciations of the American prison may be found in the proconstruction writings of John Conrad. He dismisses the moratorium as "an untenable irrelevance" but agrees with its charge that large, old prisons are not "fit for civilized habitation...." "They are," he says of fortresses like Jackson, San Quentin, and Attica, "arenas of social violence in which order is precarious and life itself is increasingly perilous for all. The megaprison is an unnatural condition for life. In no other context are people expected to live like ants in a hill, thousands of men kept in continuous proximity to one another. In these pathogenic circumstances the system controllers are justified in always expecting and preparing for the worst—murder, riot, and chaos."[51]

That imprisonment in such conditions is unjust does not require detailed demonstration. To sentence a person to imprisonment is to order him to be deprived of his liberty for a period. Specific duties in relation to his care and treatment are imposed on the prison authorities by regulation or statute, and their fulfillment can be regarded as implicit in the sentence. The additional abuse and suffering incurred in incarceration in the chaotic concrete jungles of many American corrections systems are gratuitous and unwarranted. But again, this does not resolve the question of what to do about construction—it merely raises that question.

The antibuilders also charge that sentencing is unjust. They find support, quite rightly, in the double-edged title of Marvin Frankel's *Criminal Sentences*. The former federal judge describes "a wild array of sentencing judgments without any semblance of the consistency demanded by the ideal of equal justice.... The almost wholly unchecked and sweeping powers we give to judges in the fashioning of sentences are terrifying and intolerable for a society that professes devotion to the rule of law."[52] But Frankel does not infer that no more prisons should be built, and the antibuilders are not justified in doing so. A more logical inference is that the inequities should be rectified and principles to guide sentencing developed. Some states, led in importance by California, feel they have made great progress to this end. A concern for fairness in sentencing does not lead inevitably to an anticonstruction view.

A special form of imputed injustice is racial. American prisons are disproportionately filled with the poor and the black. According to Erik Olin Wright, "During a given year, one out of every 3 to 4 black men in his early 20s spends some time in prison, in jail, on parole, or on probation, compared with about one out of every 15 white men in the same age group."[53] Police discretion, runs the argument, means that the poor and the black get arrested more frequently; judicial discretion results in the poor and the black being disproportionately sent to prison and sent for longer terms; parole discretion ensures that the poor and the black remain in prison longer. "Discretionary justice," says Milton Rector, "equals discriminatory justice against the socially powerless."[54]

We catalogue these sentiments at some length because they show the depth of the attack by the moratorium. The criticisms of new building programs are often extensions of a profound assault on the very roots of the social institution of imprisonment. These are not technical matters; they appeal to fundamental values. They cannot be accused of raising trivial or narrow issues. But their implications for construction policy are not as obvious as is sometimes claimed. It is not at all clear that the high minority concentration in prisons is due to racial discrimination by police and courts. Indeed, the evidence suggests that the explanation lies in much higher offense rates for crimes for which all citizens—of all races, and strongly among blacks—support incarceration. And even if the racial disproportion *were* due to discrimination, the logical lesson would be to correct those practices rather than refuse to lock up any criminals or to build any prisons. The notion that our society is so profoundly racist that no American criminal justice system can be fair goes well beyond the scope of this book, and probably goes beyond most antibuilders' sentiments as well. We doubt they really wish to abandon all forms of incarceration pending the arrival of a social millennium.

The Arguments for Construction

What the Public Wants

Although the public acceptability of a moratorium is seldom discussed by its supporters, the probuilders make this a central issue. In his critique of the moratorium proposals, John Conrad argues that "the general public have given no sign of accepting this revolutionary new policy." On the contrary, he found "a hard line for criminal justice" enjoying "general public approbation." Referring to the current tide of prison commitments he said, "This trend undoubtedly reflects public desire for drastic action. Sentences are becoming longer and the demand for even more severity is likely to be irresistible."[55] Offenders, he said, "are sent away from the streets because the judges sentencing them believe that the communities want that disposition. If there is evidence that severe sentencing policies are contrary to the popular will I do not see it.... We have not managed to educate the public to accept anything less than a prison sentence."[56] Given such attitudes, a cut in the use of incarceration and in the building of prisons "would severely impair confidence in the criminal justice system."[57]

James Q. Wilson has a similar basis for a proconstruction view. "Those who argue for a moratorium on new prison construction," he says, "are taking a position that is increasingly hard to understand. Since society clearly wishes its criminal laws more effectively enforced, ... this means rising prison populations, perhaps for a long period."[58] This notion is embodied nicely in the title of his article, "The Political Feasibility of Punishment."[59] But finding the proper place for public opinion is a tricky business, and we feel much less confident than these authors about our ability to divine what the American public wants. Except in the field of commerce, where evidence regarding sales is available, general statements about what the public demands may be regarded with skepticism. As Gresham Sykes puts it, "Society is a diversity, a collection of individuals with varied patterns of sentiments and behavior. And this variation is particularly marked in the area of crime and punishment."[60] In America the variations among regions, and among states within regions, and even among cities and counties within states, are large and complex. Imprisonment rates around the country reflect this, as shown in Chapter 2. So even on the assumption that penal policy should reflect public opinion, it is difficult to derive a national construction policy from the various views imputed to the amorphous beast which is society.

Moreover, how closely *should* penal policy follow public opinion? This huge question cannot be answered here, but it is worth emphasizing that the protection of everyone's rights ultimately depends on formal channels for the expression and application of that opinion. The dangers and inequities of a policy that follows too closely the shifts in vox populi are obvious enough to scare us all.

Construction and Prison Conditions

A stronger argument for construction, and a more crucial one, is that combining rising prison population with a construction moratorium subjects inmates to steadily deteriorating conditions. Wilson argues that failure to expand capacity would "brutalize the very inmates the moratorium people seek to protect,"[61] and Conrad agrees. "By standing fast on the prison moratorium," he maintains, "we preserve the filthy cages of the past for the continued misery of contemporary offenders."[62]

There is no escaping the force of this charge. Especially for liberals who disclaim any purely punitive intent, the moratorium does betray a surprising insensitivity to the plight of those who, despite fond hopes, nonetheless still wind up in prison or jail. A ban on all construction makes it virtually impossible to improve bad custodial conditions.

An equally powerful argument centers on the unfairness of the moratorium's gamble; it risks the rights and interests of real inmates today against the possibility that continued poor conditions will mean fewer inmates tomorrow. Conrad says that the proponents of the moratorium "assume that when conditions get bad enough, aroused legislators, officials, and concerned citizens will see to it that the nondangerous offenders are released so that the prison population will be reduced to a core of violent men, in number much smaller than the total capacity of the prisons they occupy." But the use of today's prisoners as pawns to reduce tomorrow's inmate populations is wrong, and is aggravated by being totally unrealistic. "All the signs," says Conrad, "indicate that the public is looking the other way."[63] Even the NCCD's Milton Rector acknowledges that "from every quarter pressures for more imprisonment are on the increase."[64]

In these circumstances, it *is* unfair for the antibuilders to recommend a course which in effect preserves the megaprison. To say, as Martinson has, "Don't build any more prisons. Tear down the ones you have,"[65] may be an understandable reaction to the appalling conditions in many prisons but does not constitute a realistic policy, or a just one. The moratorium movement will achieve only a convenient rationale for the reduction of correctional budgets. It will preserve, indeed worsen, the very institution it seeks to replace. And it uses hostages who have no voice; according to Conrad, it "will cause inevitable suffering by men, women, and children whose consent cannot be solicited or obtained."[66] He thinks this is wrong, and we think he is right.

Doing Justice and Injustice

The probuilders conclude with three arguments about justice, two good and one controversial. The controversy surrounds the link between the "justice model" of determinate sentencing and the issue of prison construction. Wilson, for example, notes the remarkable extent to which "scholars, public officials, the police and correctional officers are moving into closer agreement" on the desirability of determinate sentencing. He goes on to say that as a result more people will be locked up, and for longer periods. Thus, "a major consequence of the philosophy of just deserts is that many new, smaller, and better correctional facilities of varying kinds will have to be built.... It is the necessary implication of the position adopted by even the most liberal adherents of the just deserts philosophy."[67]

There is no doubt that in some jurisdictions determinacy could strain existing facilities. As Franklin Zimring points out in *Making the Punishment Fit the Crime,* determinate sentencing may well mean long sentences: "Once a determinate sentencing bill is before a legislative body, it takes no more than an eraser to make a one-year 'presumptive sentence' into a six-year sentence for the same offense."[68] If legislators indulge in penal inflation, judges may do so too; where fixed sentencing ranges allow any discretion, they could impose the maximum rather than the minimum permitted sentences. But to infer a proconstruction policy from these possibilities is not inevitable. Most determinate sentencing schemes—as distinct from mandatory sentencing schemes—leave judges the option of probation, so it is not certain that more people would be locked up. As for sentence length, even if it means taking their erasers away, legislators can be restrained from penal inflation if they are made to feel injustice would be done. The problem lies in deciding what constitutes an injustice, both for the offenders and the general society. By itself, the move to determinate sentencing tells us nothing about whether future prison populations will be larger or smaller than they are today.

The probuilders are persuasive with two other charges about justice. One stems from the way in which sentencing judges sometimes react to unsatisfactory prison conditions. Wilson, for example, argues that "existing facilities are . . . too lacking in amenity to enable many judges in good conscience to send offenders there."[69] Where this is true, some offenders will escape the penalty they would otherwise receive; unwilling to impose a punishment which exceeds and is irrelevant to the law's purposes, judges are forced to be erratic and thereby unjust.

A parallel injustice may be done when the availability of adequate facilities influences the time actually served, as distinct from the sentence imposed by the court. Early release achieved through liberal granting of parole or of "good time" is widely employed to reduce prison population. Federal court interventions have made this especially prevalent in recent years. Alternatively, admissions to prisons may be cut off, and sentenced state prisoners may serve their time in county jails where conditions are as bad as or worse than those found unconstitutional in the state prisons. In neither case are the ends of justice well served.

Summary Comments on the Debate

It is clear now why we described the construction debate as the tip of a policy iceberg. The construction decision is not essentially a technical exercise in matching supply to demand. On any given day, of course, that plays a part; today's commitments have to be put somewhere. But the issues are deeper than that, more intractable. It is not even obvious what new information would help. For example, some have called for more data on prisoner attitudes. But many on the right laugh at this idea, and on the left even Rector says that "our moral obligation is to act in accordance with our belief, not to distribute questionnaires."[70] Is it possible, or right, to determine the best interests of those confined without consulting them? The moratorium is bargaining the interests of today's many prisoners against the hope that in future there will be fewer. We believe it is a gamble no outside critic has a right to try to impose, but this is a judgment difficult to make more forceful by the marshaling of new facts.

The arguments for and against construction cover a huge range. Two types of concern weave in and out in an intellectual do-si-do. They can be loosely identified as quantitative (concern about population size, space, and conditions) and qualitative (consideration of the purposes of imprisonment, the proper standards of justice and ethics, and so on). There are really two debates being conducted, usually without much contact with each other. Among policymakers, the quantitative debate has dominated and is important enough to require further comment.

Because of the complexity and unpleasantness of the subject, society has tended to leave the problem of prison conditions to those who have direct responsibility for it: corrections commissioners, prison wardens and jail administrators, parole boards, and the occasional legislative subcommittee. These officials tend to concentrate on counting heads, and given their mission one should not expect more. For example, in an article warning of future riots unless crowding is relieved, the executive director of the American Correctional Association asserts, "We are not debating the pros and cons of incarceration."[71] This uncritical acceptance of traditional premises sharply limits the contribution of professional administrators to the policy debate.

The wave of judicial intervention has added a dimension, but the courts too have concentrated on the physical aspects of the problem and have been reluctant to enter the qualitative or purposes debate. Although this judicial restraint could erode in the future, we certainly cannot count on it, and in any case the judiciary is not the proper source of such normative policy. But if the debate on imprisonment is left to those parts of government with direct operational responsibility for it, concentration on the physical aspect is likely to prevail.

Another development could be even worse. Correctional administrators could try to deal with the qualitative issues without debating them in a public forum. There is some evidence that this is already occurring. Perhaps in despair over getting elected officials to face the difficult questions, perhaps feeling that they are the real experts, perhaps through normal bureaucratic momentum, correctional administrators have begun to make both pronouncements and policies on some fundamental matters. In Minnesota, the corrections department tries to induce local jurisdictions to send fewer inmates to state facilities.[72] In New York, a recent commissioner proposed that thirteen- and fourteen-year-old offenders, who are now held in juvenile facilities, be incarcerated in adult prisons.

Whatever one's view of these substantive proposals, we feel they reflect an unwelcome trend. The questions of whom to imprison, for how long, and for what purposes ought not to be left to appointed prison officials, however humane and well-intentioned they may be. These are questions of the deepest political and ethical significance. The proper responses to the limitations of specialized officials is not to broaden the responsibility of those officials but rather to broaden the debate itself to include the right participants. In this regard, federal, state, and local legislatures bear heavy responsibilities which they do not always discharge. On issues such as who should go to prison and why, the difficult but proper role of correctional administrators is simply to respond to legislative leads applied by sentencing courts. Some officials chafe under this restraint and have coined the term "proactive" to express their wish for a role that does more than react. In our view, this is neither a proper nor a desirable expansion of their mission.

A special drawback in leaving this debate to administrators is the officials' excessive reliance on forecasts and projections. Flowing from the concentration on the measurable, and from the view of the problem as an exercise in supply and demand, is the idea that the demand can somehow be predicted. Almost every corrections department in the country prepares detailed forecasts of the future size of the correctional population and makes construction and other plans accordingly. As noted in our preface, the Congress directed the U.S. Department of Justice to forecast prison populations state by state, year by year.[73] Sometimes such projections are used to support policy conclusions already reached, but often they have an independent influence. Sometimes officials really believe the numbers.

A *New Yorker* cartoon once portrayed two cavemen commiserating about the difficulty of "controlling pregnancy when we don't know what causes it." In correctional policy, we are better off than the cavemen. We know where prison populations come from, and it's not from the stork. They are the result of literally millions of decisions made throughout the criminal justice system, including the legislatures which pass penal laws. The diffuse character of these decisions, and the uncertain grounds on which they are based, make long-term projection virtually useless except to illustrate the consequences of a particular set of choices. Fancy forecasting techniques will not tell us much about either the likely or the preferred future of American imprisonment. If long-range predictions turned out to be very accurate, it would be by accident. But despite this, specialists and administrators like to use them, and two dangers are created.

The first is the danger of false confidence. We have seen that two national commissions drew their views on prison construction from low projections of the prison population. The 1973 commission used low numbers to justify a recommendation for a ten-year moratorium.[74] Although the commission was attracted to this proposal on broader ideological grounds, there seems little doubt that the optimistic forecast had an independent influence. That forecast, of course, was invalidated in the very year it was published; 1973 was the year in which the total national prison population began its steep rise. The false confidence in the low projection led to an overly relaxed attitude on the part of many administrators. In particular, it produced a refusal to see warning signs, such as rising incarceration rates, and thus left administrators vulnerable to surprise. Exactly this happened to most corrections departments in the mid-1970s.

A related pitfall is that false confidence may become self-fulfilling prophecy. In those states where population levels are influenced by the availability of space, an unwarranted confidence in high-population projections may prove accurate simply because it leads to the creation of new capacity which automatically gets used. Although some officials use these projections cynically, to support construction plans they would pursue anyway, others are simply following the dictates of the forecasters. Moreover, the situation is not reciprocal; confidence in low-population projections seldom results in closing facilities and reducing capacity. There may be an artificial floor under population size, but no ceiling.

The indiscriminate use of projections can lend itself to parody, such as the sage forecast that by the year 2020 everyone in the United States will be working for the Post Office. Projections clarify the implications of a current or proposed course, but they must not be used as a predictive basis for action. To do so is a trap, because it makes the policy process seem less complex and more mechanical than it really is. As we suggest by this book's title, the future of imprisonment must be chosen rather than predicted. Sheldon Wolin has discovered that the Chinese language has no single character to represent our concept of crisis, but two: one means danger, and the other means opportunity. They might be describing American prison policy over the next few years.

2 The Numbers Game

A prison policy or, more accurately, an imprisonment practice is society's answer to a three-part question: who should be locked up, for how long, under what conditions? It should be obvious that each part of the inquiry is ultimately normative. Yet on each aspect of the question, the contemporary debate is frequently not an inquiry into social norms but a search for a mythical magic number. Unfortunately, neither appropriate inmate population nor optimal sentence length nor acceptable prison conditions can be divined in a moral and political vacuum. To do so was never really possible, even in the days of relative consensus on prison purposes and standards. An attempt is almost ludicrous now that the consensus has dissolved.

In this field, quantitative analyses can have policy lessons only if they are related explicitly to the controversy over purposes and ethics. Otherwise, the meticulous counting of prisoners, square feet, time served, decibels, etc., becomes a mechanical and dubious exercise. Prison population is too large or too small and prison conditions too harsh or too comfortable only in comparison to competing social values. Numbers do not, as is often claimed, speak for themselves. The accumulation of data, no matter how sophisticated the measurement techniques, cannot by itself yield a policy.

The report of the 1967 Crime Commission illustrates the point. As we have shown, the commission considered prison crowding only in passing, as a feature of a few facilities or as a result of past growth in correctional populations. It expressed no dismay that the national inmate total had "decreased about one percent per year in the past few years, despite increases in the total population of the country *and in serious crime*" (emphasis added). It noted with apparent approval that "the courts are making increased use of alternatives to commitment at the adult level."[1] This impression is reinforced by the panel's recommendations, which stress the possibilities of diversion from traditional incarcerative institutions. The commission's Task Force on Corrections and its professional staff were favorably impressed by the then recent California innovations of adult probation subsidy and the juvenile Community Treatment Program. An emphasis on problems of prison crowding might easily have distracted attention from such innovations. It might also have stimulated a new call for prison construction, which was the last thing the commission wanted to encourage.

The authors of the 1967 report were humane, intelligent people. Looking at the data, they discerned a move in some adult corrections systems away from traditional policies, and they liked this result. They saw building more prisons to be part of the problem, not part of the solution. But looking at these same data, observers with different ideologies and values inferred quite different policies. Some felt the commission was too easily satisfied by existing housing conditions, which were known to be poor in many state and local facilities. A much larger group felt the commission was insufficiently outraged by two trends which intersected like blades of a scissors; a sustained rise in serious crime was being accompanied by a decline in prison population. Conservatives argued that this was not only unjust, it was unpopular. They pointed to opinion surveys, which showed increasing support for harsher treatment of criminals, to bolster their claim that something was wrong with America's policy. Just as 1960s liberals found it obvious that no more prisons should be built, so 1960s conservatives found it obvious that more construction money was absolutely necessary.

These polarized interpretations of a single body of data have persisted to the present. In 1973, after the national prison population had stopped declining and started rising, the National Advisory Commission said, "The facts lead logically to the conclusion that no new institutions for adults should be built and existing institutions for juveniles should be closed." Except in rare instances, the commission said, public policy should be "a 10-year moratorium on construction of institutions."[2] And as the rate of population increase rose through the mid-1970s, this opposition to construction did not abate but actually intensified in some quarters; the formal establishment of the National Moratorium, for example, coincided with the decade's peak pressure applied by new commitments on existing capacity.

Then, as now, these policy recommendations flowed not "logically" from the facts, as the commission claimed, but from political and social values. Now as then, it remains impossible to reach policy conclusions directly from numbers. But the equivocal lessons of data analysis do not justify ignoring it. In this chapter, we shall try to show both the limitations and uses of the quantitative analyses we have lumped under the unflattering rubric of the numbers game.

Numbers and History

The past, recent and distant, provides a rich vein of numbers which can be mined according to the analyst's preferences. The national head-count is a prominent example. Headlines report with satisfied alarm that "U.S. Prison Population Hits All-Time High," and articles trumpet that the United States began a particular year "with more people in prison than ever before in the nation's history."[3] But depending on one's ideological preferences, such historical comparisons can be read in more than one way. They are sometimes taken to indicate that the prison problem is worse than ever before, although recent annual increments are not unprecedented,[4] and almost half of the past fifty years began with record numbers of inmates. More pertinent is that such comparisons over time are meaningless unless these head-counts are related to something else. Ultimately, judgments about size imply deep social and ethical choices about how sanctions should be distributed among citizens. No simple set of numbers will tell us whether public safety is improved by maintaining a particular number of prisoners, much less whether the improvement is large enough to justify the cost, both human and fiscal, of continued imprisonment. In the absence of such standards, analysts have turned to the capacity of the facilities and the size of the general population (the latter yielding the imprisonment rate) as two points of reference in interpreting the significance of the size of the inmate population.

Historical comparisons of inmate population and institutional capacity constitute an especially frustrating feature of the numbers game. As we have noted, successive generations of policymakers keep rediscovering the same problem. Certainly, today's views of insufficient capacity are not unprecedented; since the inception of the penitentiary, complaints about overpopulation have been a persistent feature of penal history. Among many others, Rush and Eddy complained in the eighteenth century, Beaumont and Tocqueville in the nineteenth. McKelvey's survey of the entire institution reads like a catalog of what today's commentators, in an unfortunate turn of phrase, call "crowding crunches." The most important inquiry in the first half of the twentieth century simply continued the litany; in 1931 the Wickersham Commission concluded that with "the present overcrowded conditions" the prison system had not only failed to protect society but also "contributes to the increase of crime by hardening the prisoner."[5]

After presenting Census Bureau figures that showed overcrowding in prisons and reformatories for 1927 as 19 percent more than original capacity, the Wickersham report went on to say that "the present situation [in 1931] is unquestionably worse than it was in 1927 and is probably worse than it has ever been, taking the country as a whole."[6] As the population of the state and federal prisons and reformatories rose by 28 percent in those four years, it seems likely that the situation had deteriorated. Whether it was worse than it had ever been cannot be determined because the first nationwide collection of prison data was not made by the Bureau of the Census until 1926.

The national data did not really make historical comparisons easier. In 1939, for example, a major study by Fred Haynes described "serious overcrowding" as one of the "twin evils in American penal institutions." "In the majority of prisons," he wrote, "the population is 50 to 100 percent above the normal capacity." The other evil he saw as subordinate; it was "lack of employment," which he said "naturally results from overcrowding."[7] Although the data do not permit detailed comparisons over longer periods of history, it is generally clear that widely varying amounts of space and types of conditions could be included in Haynes's notion of overcrowding. The degree of outrage or satisfaction expressed by any observer depended on standards of his day and on personal penal philosophy. While not usually as candid as the nineteenth-century Auburn inspectors who sought "dread and terror," those who regarded prisons as places of punishment were generally more tolerant of crowding than those who emphasized rehabilitation.

In all eras, diverging ideological perspectives have made it hazardous to infer a prison policy directly from measurements of crowding. Crowding, after all, is a psychological condition, and different cultures have lived with widely varying standards of personal space. The effects of proximity depend on the attitudes and behavior of the people who are being crowded as much as on their physical conditions. How much space is required depends on what society feels is deserved, just, humane, and so on. These terms are hardly self-defining. To see crowding as an excess of population over capacity begs the question of what capacity should be ascribed to a physical housing unit, and telescopes quantitative and qualitative judgments about how many inmates a particular prison can hold.

Thus, when today's debaters try to compare crowding levels over time the result is analytic chaos. This is especially true because the American concept of capacity has been so flexible—a charitable adjective—as to render it useless for historical comparisons. Even now, it can be dangerous unless carefully specified. But since the population/capacity ratio is a central part of the contemporary debate, it must be reviewed in some detail.

Table 2.1
Difference between Rated Capacity and Prison Population (March 31, 1978)

Facilities	Rated Capacity	Prison Population	Deficiency in Capacity
Federal	22,800	29,700	6,900
State	254,600	258,900	4,300
U.S. total	277,400	288,600	11,200

SOURCE: Abt Associates, "American Prisons and Jails," vol. 3, "Conditions and Costs of Confinement," 1979 draft, unpublished.

Consider the data in table 2.1 for 1978, the latest year for which national aggregates of both capacity and population were available. Prima facie these figures represent a considerably lower level of overcrowding than that found by the Wickersham Commission—only 4 percent excess of population over capacity in 1978 as compared to 19.1 percent in 1931. This, however, is precisely the picture the raters of capacity wished to present to the world. The administrators of corrections systems were under no constraint in determining how many people could occupy each room in their institutions. If four people actually lived in a cell, then clearly its capacity—in the lexical sense of maximum ability to contain—must be at least four. As long as the corrections department was not seeking additional space, there was little incentive to report statistics which suggested that it might be operating in violation of its own standards. Because of the equivocal nature of the concept of capacity and the absence of a standard definition for it in either period, the comparison is of little significance. Making calculations of this nature is analogous to the practice of John Dewey's Texas farmer, who weighed his pigs by putting them on one end of a plank that was balanced in the middle, placing rocks on the plank's other end until it was level, and then guessing the weight of the rocks.

Why do we make this unflattering comparison? In the first place, although it is hardly a novel insight to see that rated capacity is a flexible concept, failure to bear this in mind has frustrated previous attempts to define the extent of the problem. Thus, the estimate of total rated capacity shown in table 2.1 was derived from estimates provided by managements of individual institutions or by the central corrections agencies in the various states. Institutions and agencies differ in the way in which they calculate rated capacity, and a variety of political, legal, and financial considerations may influence them.

But even when no such considerations are involved, statements about capacity which refer to the ability to accommodate human beings differ significantly from capacity statements which might refer to the ability to store goods. It is true that physical capacity can be measured in cubic feet of space. But people are not packing cases and while living, at any rate, require more than the space measured in cubic units into which they can be compressed.

The problem is that when the question, "How much more?" is asked, it raises considerations that are outside the field of objectively measurable phenomena. For when the concept of capacity relates to the accommodation of people, it involves more than physical features that are observable and verifiable. Determining the capacity of a building to provide human habitation or living quarters will of course involve the consideration of physical features, but implicit in all judgments about the ability of a structure to house human beings are also considerations of value, decisions about sufficiency or adequacy involving a different kind of measurement.

Consider, for example, Orlando Lewis, general secretary of the American Prison Association, writing in the early 1920s about the cells in Sing Sing. He described them as "intolerably small, often very damp, and altogether unfit for human habitation." He also wrote of "the pernicious 'doubling up' of prisoners in these viciously small cells in a great, damp, bastille-like structure."[8] The dampness, he observed, was due to the fact that the prison was, incorrectly, sited at the water's edge. The cells were seven feet long, three feet three inches wide, and six feet seven inches high.

A hundred years before, the commissioners who were responsible for building Sing Sing took a very different view. They certainly did not feel they had been niggardly in the provision of cell space. Indeed, they pointed out to the legislature in 1826 that by hanging the iron-grated cell doors flush with the corridor rather than nearly two feet back at the inner end of the cell door recess, as was done at Auburn prison, they had enabled the prisoner "when pacing up and down within his cell [to] extend his walk from two and a half steps to three steps."[9]

Far from thinking the location of the prison unsuitable, the commissioners were delighted with the site. "A more healthy situation could not have been selected,"[10] they said. Their views on the practice of doubling up are not recorded, but the practice was begun at the outset of the prison's history. Indeed, before the prison was completed, convicts were already being housed two in a cell. It was not until nearly a century later that this "pernicious" practice became a major issue in a campaign for the abolition of Sing Sing. Nor is this merely a matter of historical relativity, for the differences of opinion may well be contemporaneous. For example, when William Crawford was sent by the British to visit Sing Sing in 1832, his report on the cells was no less critical than Orlando Lewis's nearly a century later.[11] And the American reformer Dorothea Dix, who visited the prison in 1845, was equally condemnatory.[12] Both observers, incidentally, noted the dampness of the cells and attributed this to the unsuitable location of the prison.

One factor which was, and clearly should be, considered relevant to the determination of cell size was the nature of the prison regime. Cellular provisions in America were more generous in prisons modeled on the Eastern State Penitentiary in Philadelphia, which was designed for the continuous separate and solitary confinement of inmates, than in prisons like Sing Sing, which was modeled on Auburn prison and designed for solitary confinement only during the night. Even so, later commentators like Barnes and Teeters remark that "the cells at Auburn and Sing Sing were ridiculously small, being unfit for human habitation even during nonworking hours."[13]

Because of the essential relativity of the concept of capacity, it is not surprising that rated capacity should have proved extremely adaptable. Recognition of this led the Bureau of the Census in 1937 to cease its routine comparison of prison population with what was then termed *normal capacity*. The bureau gave the following explanation:

> In past reports there have been presented data showing the "normal capacity" of the institutions as compared with the average daily population. This information was again reported by the institutions for 1937, but because of difficulty in defining "normal capacity" it has seemed best not to publish these data again. In the absence of a standard formula for the determination of normal capacity of a penal institution, it is likely, for example, that one institution with 1,000 cells and 2,000 prisoners may report a normal capacity on the basis of one man to a cell making it appear that the institution is badly overcrowded, with the population equal to 200 percent of its capacity, while another institution, of the same size and population, may report normal capacity on the basis of two men to a cell, with the result that no overcrowding would be indicated. Certainly, where different types of institutions report these data, the difficulty of obtaining any comparable figures on capacity is greatly increased. It appears almost impossible to determine on any uniform basis what would be the "normal capacity" of institutions such as prison farms and camps.[14]

The role of these ambiguities in balancing supply and demand is illustrated by James Jacobs's excellent history of Stateville Penitentiary in Illinois.[15] When the institution opened in 1925, it was built to accommodate 1,392 inmates; most of the cells were approximately sixty square feet and were designed to hold a single inmate. In practice, at one time (in 1935) it housed 3,952 inmates. Over the years it appears that there have been no major additions to the institution's physical dimensions, but rated capacity has been adjusted to population accommodation requirements. At the time of the U.S. government's survey in 1978, the rated capacity was given as 2,700, which accorded coincidentally with a ceiling imposed by a federal court. The actual population of the institution at that time was 2,678, which meant that the penitentiary had an excess of rated capacity over prison population. In fact, however, the population was nearly twice the size for which the institution was originally intended.[16]

Thus, rated capacity can be taken to mean design capacity or original capacity (the phrase used in the Wickersham Commission report), which refers to the number of inmates the architect intended to house. It might be used in this way when, as a result of population pressure, funds were being sought to provide additional accommodation. Or, as in the case of the early Bureau of the Census reports, it can mean normal capacity, which appears to have signified whatever reporting institutions wanted it to signify. Similarly, in more recent years the use of rated capacity has enabled correctional officials to represent similar facilities in different jurisdictions as possessing dramatically different capacities. It can also be interpreted as meaning operational capacity or present capacity, this including parts of the institution not originally intended as accommodation areas but converted into living space to cope with increased population. Alternatively, it might be construed in terms of optimum capacity as defined by a court order, by the National Clearing House for Criminal Justice Planning and Architecture, or by some other authority, such as the Federal Bureau of Prisons.

Citizens in general and legislators in particular must understand the games that interested parties may and do play with numbers that purport to indicate whether prison capacity is exceeded and new construction required. The manifest dangers of using such elastic terms should lead policymakers to examine such calculations carefully and should lead analysts to look for measures with some sort of physical objectivity.

Beyond Flexible Capacity

One such measure is the number of inmates who have a room (of whatever size) to themselves. This standard dates back to the beginning of the modern penitentiary system. When John Howard made his famous report on *The State of the Prisons* in England in 1777, he expressed his horror at the "scenes of calamity" and especially at the indiscriminate mingling of all classes of prisoners. "I wish all prisoners to have separate rooms,"[17] he said, and these were possibly the most influential words he ever wrote. When the first inspectors of prisons were appointed in the early nineteenth century, their reports strongly advocated cellular isolation. Indeed, the British government seems "to have judged all prisons according to the degree in which [the] practice of separate cells was adopted."[18] In America, the Philadelphia Society for Alleviating the Miseries of Public Prisons, from its founding in 1787, was in direct contact with Howard. The designers of the Pennsylvania separate system freely acknowledged their debt to this great British reformer.

The historical bias in favor of single-celling, of course, is not enough to justify holding the system to this standard. We may distinguish four reasons why the rule of one man–one cell might be reasonable; our view is that although traditional justifications may have weakened, another has emerged which justifies single-celling as a basic determinant of the level of prison crowding.

Weaker in the late twentieth century than in the late eighteenth is the claim that single-celling is necessary to prevent prisons from becoming schools for crime. In today's world, this argument has considerable force when applied to classification (separate prisons for different types of inmates), but is probably unworkable within a particular institution. Twentieth-century America is not going to return to either the solitary system of nineteenth-century Pennsylvania or the silent system of nineteenth-century Auburn. Therefore, today's inmate will have ample opportunity to learn new criminal skills from his colleagues even if he has a private room in which to sleep. The "schools for crime" theory is not sufficient basis for mandating the standard of the single cell. Nor can long-abandoned hopes for introspection and penitence support such a high and expensive standard.

The contemporary prison, however, has other features which more than justify the rule of one man–one cell; when a citizen is convicted of a crime, he may be deprived of his liberty for a period of time (often all too loosely specified) and may be forced to give up other rights to assure the orderly and secure administration of the prison. After his release, he may forfeit rights and privileges concerning voting, professional certification, and so on. But beyond this, he retains the rights with which he entered. The extent to which a right to privacy might entitle him to a single cell is controversial and has not yet been fully resolved by the appellate courts. The trend of federal decisions has been to deny any absolute right to privacy, instead balancing the prisoner's interest in privacy against other administrative requirements on the institution (in *Forts v. Ward*).[19] The Supreme Court has said, "There is no one-man-one-cell rule lurking in the constitution" (*Bell v. Wolfish*),[20] clearly establishing that, for legal purposes at least, the totality of conditions of confinement must determine whether a prisoner's rights have been violated. However, there is no doubt that in many prisons at many times the threats to personal safety when prisoners are forced to share sleeping accommodations with others constitute cruel and unusual punishment, and as such violate constitutional protections. The court-imposed sentence did not carry with it the dangers of being beaten, raped, and terrorized. It is naive to deny that violence of various kinds is endemic in many American prisons. This, we maintain, is sufficient grounds for making one man–one cell a standard to which the American prison system should be held. A prison can fairly be called overcrowded whenever it fails this test.

The acceptance of single-celling in principle, however, does little more than set a partial, theoretical standard. Insofar as institutions have opted for separation, and have resorted to the creation of dormitories or to double and even triple-celling only under population pressure, the extent to which prisoners are confined in multi-occupied cells provides a legitimate measure of crowding. Unfortunately, it is a measure of only one dimension of crowding, for it ignores the possibility that where single occupancy prevails the inmates so accommodated may be confined in very constricted conditions. We have noted, for example, that as late as the 1920s Sing Sing had many cells with less than twenty-five square feet of floor space. Even to begin an assessment of whether a prison is overcrowded, we need not only the number of inmates but also the number of square feet inside the cells. In recent years, the corrections literature has displayed a rash of competing standards. The National Advisory Commission on Criminal Justice Standards and Goals recommended in 1973 that institutions "should provide for privacy and personal space by the use of single rooms with a floor area of at least 80 square feet per man."[21] This view was accepted by the 1977 Commission on Accreditation for Corrections and the 1978 Department of Justice draft "Federal Standards for Corrections." Other existing standards are somewhat lower, ranging from seventy-five square feet per inmate (Federal Bureau of Prisons) and seventy square feet (National Clearing House for Criminal Justice Planning and Architecture and the National Sheriffs' Association) to sixty-five square feet (United Nations Minimum Standards) and sixty square feet (American Correctional Association).[22]

By historical standards, these ideals appear reasonable but no better. The floor area recommended by the National Advisory Commission in 1973, the most spacious of the suggested standards, is precisely the same as that recommended in *Extract and Remarks on the Subject of Punishment and Reformation of Criminals*, which was published by the Philadelphia Society for Alleviating the Miseries of Public Prisons in 1790.[23] It is considerably less than what was actually provided in the first half of the nineteenth century at, for example, the Eastern State Penitentiary in Philadelphia (96 sq ft) or at

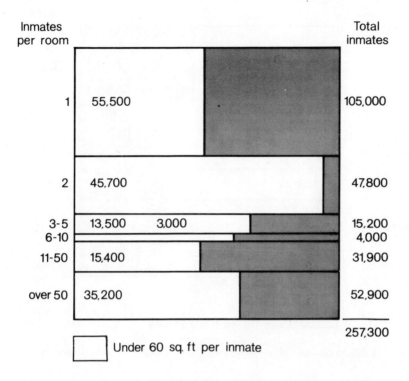

FIGURE 2.1: Single and multiple occupancy and crowding: state and local prisons. Source: Data from Abt Associates, *American Prisons and Jails*, vol. 3, *Conditions and Costs of Confinement* (Washington, D.C.: National Institute of Justice, 1980).

Pentonville Prison in London, England (91 sq ft). (In both cases the cells were designed for solitary confinement.)

More pertinent is that most American inmates do not actually enjoy such "luxury." The 1978 federal study found that only 37 percent of the inmates of American prisons and jails enjoyed the privacy of a single room, and that 66 percent have fewer than the sixty square foot minimum prescribed by most standard setting bodies. A particularly unfortunate 46 percent found themselves sharing with other inmates units so small that they provided less than sixty square feet per person. Only 17 percent actually achieved John Howard's standard of a separate room with the sixty square feet of modern standard-setters. The sharing of space reflected in these data is not merely double occupancy of single rooms. The survey found multiple occupancies in facilities around the country, where inmates had as little as twenty square feet per person. Figures 2.1 and 2.2 portray the national distribution of inmates by number of prisoners and available floor space.

Despite the fact that housing for 83 percent of state inmates fails to

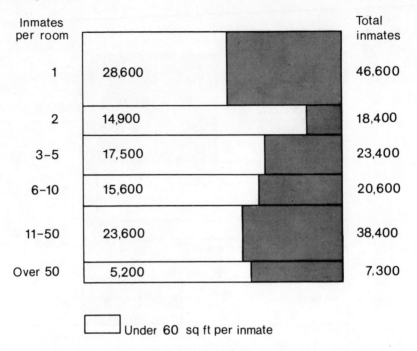

FIGURE 2.2: Single and multiple occupancy and crowding: local jails. Source: See fig. 2.1.

meet one of our basic crowding standards, state departments of correction reported in the aggregate a rated capacity only 4,300 units below their actual population. This can only mean that the standards on which their ratings were based were vastly different from those we have described. Abt Associates computed the numbers of inmates who could be housed to meet at least one of the space/occupancy standards (i.e., *either* a single room *or* 60 sq ft). Table 2.2 shows that approximately 45,000 state prisoners (and 8,000 in the federal prisons) would have to be released (or an equivalent number of new units built) to achieve these standards.

This analysis should inspire, if nothing else, an appreciation of the chapter's title. If one plays the game of rated capacity, in which the rules are so flexible, the aggregate picture of the state prisons is not so bad: the system is overcrowded by only 1.7 percent. If, however, one plays by fixed rules and combined capacity measures, then the system is in some sense ten times more overcrowded. We acknowledge that there are many attributes of the physical and personal space of confinement which makes its conditions more or less tolerable. An inmate's sense of privacy and physical security, access to communications and visual stimuli, lighting, noise, and air quality all

Table 2.2
Deficiency in Capacity by Rated Capacity and Combined Measure Capacity (1978)

Facilities	Prison Population	Deficiency	
		Rated Capacity	Capacity
Federal	29,700	6,900	8,000
State	258,900	4,300	45,000
U.S. total	288,600	11,200	53,000

SOURCE: See table 2.1.

may contribute to the psychological impact of physical confinement. While the two measures discussed above are widely recognized as important, they do not completely characterize the prison environment. They do, however, permit relatively reliable measurement, and recent data are available on the available space and occupancy levels of most institutions in the United States. From this perspective, the system taken as a whole is struggling and generally failing to meet a fair and reasonable standard of prison crowding.

Numbers and Level of Analysis

Does it make sense to speak of America's prisons "taken as a whole"? Although aggregations of statistics at the national level can be useful to suggest dimensions of the problem, they can also be misleading and therefore risky for the policymaker. National aggregates, after all, do not reflect the organization of the inmates or the administrative and legislative units that determine their fate. There is no American correctional system; there are fifty state prisons systems, one federal prison system, and 3,400 local jail systems. These are run by separate bureaucracies according to largely different procedures governed by different bodies of legislation.

This fragmentation means that gross national figures may be extremely deceptive. In the simplest case, a year in which the national aggregate of inmates remained unchanged from the previous year could be taken to mean that nothing much is happening in the trend of American prison population. Yet a net of small or zero change may mask extreme shifts in individual systems. In the preliminary figures for *Corrections Magazine*'s 1981 count of prisoners, for example, a modest 5.5 percent increase is reported for the national aggregate. At least half of this could easily be statistical noise, making the national statement even less striking. But when the aggregate is broken down, some very significant shifts both up and down can be discerned. Over a third of the states reported increases of more than twice the national average rate, while one quarter showed no growth or even decreasing populations. And, we emphasize, inmates do not live in nationally aggregated conditions; a prisoner in one state is not less crowded because another state has empty cells.

This point, incidentally, induces further wariness about historical comparisons of national crowding levels. The Wickersham Commission report, for example, which produced a national overcrowding percentage of 19 for 1927, did so by collating figures from states in widely divergent situations. Even allowing for noncomparability of capacity definitions, Michigan reported 79 percent more inmates than capacity, California 62 percent, Oklahoma 57 percent. But other states were suffering, if that is the term, from severe undercrowding: New Hampshire reported an excess of 52 percent capacity over total inmate population, Montana 39 percent, Utah 30 percent.[24] Thus, in formulating a national perspective, little significance can be attached to the arithmetic mean of a series composed of such highly variant quantities.

Some commentators acknowledge this, but then proceed to another dubious exercise: the aggregation of prison data according to Census Bureau regions. It is difficult to assess the significance of these. They do make clear that the overcrowding problem is not a national one, in that it is not distributed throughout every part of the nation in the same degree. Although it is true that almost all states experienced rising prison populations in the mid-1970s, the prison overpopulation problem clearly did not extend uniformly throughout the nation. In most significant respects, the crucial regional difference is that between the South and the rest of the United States. To some observers, these data are intrinsically interesting and provocative. Almost half of all state inmates are in institutions in the South. The South has a substantially larger proportion of prison inmates than its share of the general national population, whereas the other three regions all have proportions of prison inmates lower than their respective shares of the general population. Half of the inmates of state prisons are drawn from about one-third of the United States population.

Regional comparisons show. also that prison conditions are substantially more crowded in the South than in other regions. The South contributes a grossly disproportionate share to the one-half of all inmates in the United States who live in crowded or high-density, multiple-occupancy confinement. Whereas 60 percent of the inmates in Southern state facilities live in those conditions, in the Northeast, only 5 percent do so. Nearly half of the state cells in the South confine at least two inmates compared with only 16 percent in the North Central region, 7 percent in the West, and 1 percent in the Northeast.

Table 2.3 shows four indices of crowded living conditions. In each

Table 2.3
Regional Distribution of Crowding (1978)

% Inmates with:	Northeast	North Central	South	West
Multiple occupancy	16	45	83	44
Less than 60 sq ft	53	54	77	60
Both measures	12	31	67	20
Dormitory housing[a]	4	19	48	28

SOURCE: See table 2.1.
[a]More than 10 prisoners per room.

respect the South far exceeds the rest of the United States. Five of every six Southern prisoners live in multiple occupancy units, half of them in dormitory units housing more than ten inmates. In the Northeast, only one-sixth of the prisoners share their cells, and dormitory housing is rare. Two-thirds of Southern inmates have the worst of both measures: the facilities they occupy have substandard areas and must be shared with other prisoners. In no other region is the rate of high-density, multiple-occupancy housing even half as great.

In figure 2.3 we see the level of crowding in each of the state corrections systems. The worst offenders are: Texas (90%), North Carolina (84%), Mississippi and South Carolina (78%), Florida (72%), and New Mexico (68%). The only Southern state in the less-crowded half of the distribution is Delaware, in which a federal judge had ordered the release of inmates a year earlier after finding conditions in the state penitentiary to be unconstitutionally cruel.

One may speculate, of course, on the causes of regional variations in prison conditions and incarceration rates. Is the Southern prison attributable to some residue of the institution of slavery, or to the expansible capacity of the plantation-style prisons, or to some other influence? These are interesting questions, well beyond the scope of this inquiry. But more to the point is that, at the regional level, even the answers would be of doubtful usefulness to the policymaker. There is no regional correctional system, anymore than there is a national system. The regional perspective is of greater interest to the sociologist or cultural anthropologist than to the legislator deciding whether to fund more prison construction.

An argument can be made, we suppose, that regional disparities should increase the perceived need for federal intervention in state imprisonment policy and practice. In this view, the regional clustering of high imprisonment rates and high crowding rates reflects a deep cultural tradition which will be very hard to change by gentle persuasion, and which requires major pressure from the top down. Both Northern and Southern liberals find this view attractive, and

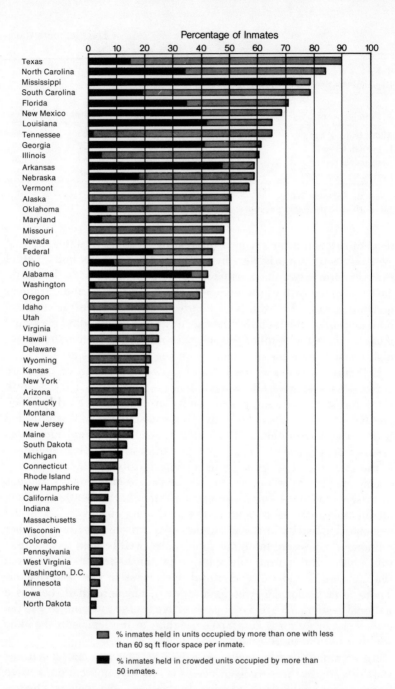

FIGURE 2.3: Percentage of inmates held in crowded confinement units in state and federal correctional facilities by state (March 31, 1978). A "crowded" confinement unit is a cell or dormitory with two or more inmates and less than 60 sq ft of floor space per inmate. Source: Abt Associates data from "Survey of State and Federal Adult Correctional Facilities," unpublished.

some version of it may play a part in the intervention of federal courts in state prison administrations. But to us, it hardly seems sufficient to justify extensive attention to regional data on the prison problem.

In the minds of some observers, the regional data are important to dramatize the unpleasant correlation of high imprisonment rates, high crowding levels, and a high percentage of racial minorities in the general population. In this view, region and race are inseparable in thinking about the prison problem. As William Nagel[25] and others have shown, one of the strongest correlations in the numbers game is between a state's imprisonment rate and its racial composition. States with a high percentage of black citizens tend to have substantially higher imprisonment rates than states which rank lower. This is especially disturbing in the absence of other, "commonsense" correlations. One common view is that punishment, in the form of high incarceration rates, is the inevitable consequence of crime, which is presumed to correlate with the presence of minority populations. But Nagel found that states with high fractions of nonwhite citizens on average had slightly lower crime rates than other states. Moreover, there was no tendency for states with high crime rates to have high imprisonment rates. This last is sometimes taken by political conservatives as evidence that the threat of imprisonment deters crime, but Carlson and others have shown convincingly that, in most jurisdictions over time, crime and imprisonment rates simply have little to do with each other. The cross-national comparison in the next chapter further undermines this commonsense connection.

This demonstration, incidentally, suggests grounds for pessimism about the link between the numbers game and the purposes debate. By one standard of proof, Nagel's work should undercut the institution of imprisonment because it can be shown to be neither responding to or controlling crime. However, the fact that imprisonment rates are rising or remaining high at a time when understanding of its ineffectiveness is spreading suggests that something other than a search for such effectiveness is driving the institution. If the analysis in Chapter 4 is correct, much of its intractability is easily understood. Whatever is causing it, traditional legalism may be more deeply ingrained in some parts of the country than others and will remain a strong bulwark against revisionists who are seeking change.

If masking accurate descriptions were the worst feature of national and regional perspectives, this would not be very serious. The country can survive a modest increase in the number of articles that do not advance the occult science of policymaking. But in fact the national perspective can be dangerous. As indicated in Chapter 1, if the U.S. Congress decides that prison crowding constitutes a national crisis, and (in our view, mistakenly) concludes also that this can be rectified with a national building program, certain federal initiatives may be taken that would be avoided if the system were regarded from the bottom up. Unintended and possibly unpleasant consequences may follow. In our view, the greatest risk is in dispensing federal construction money which is insufficiently tailored to states' specific situations. The mechanism for this could be as simple as the application of a poorly conceived federal funding formula. In some states, liberal fears may be justified that building more capacity simply means having a larger, and not less crowded, prison population.

A review of the literature shows that surprisingly little has been done even to test this hypothesis. So far as we are aware, the only statistical work that examines the question is that of Kenneth Carlson. As part of the 1978 Justice Department survey, Carlson constructed a national-level model to examine the correlations of new construction and population movements after 1955. He concluded that *(a)* there is no relation between future capacities and present populations; that is, the system does not seem to be building its capacity to deal with the inmates already in custody. It is not simply making the necessary adjustments to increments in a long-term upward population trend. *(b)* There is also no relation between capacity change and population change in the same year or with a one-year lag. However, *(c)* there *is* a significant, substantial (approximately one inmate per unit of space) effect of past capacity changes on future populations. Thus, this study maintains that on the average "capacities do not appear to be changed more often in crowded conditions than at other times; new space is filled to rated capacity by the second year after opening the additional space; within five years, the occupancy of the new space averages 130 percent of rated capacity."[26]

Carlson acknowledged that some states in some years showed less responsive behavior while others showed more, and he emphasized that "these are aggregate historical statistical trends, and not rigid rules governing the behavior of every state." Nonetheless, his work can fairly be taken as support—not proof, certainly not for a particular state[27]—for the notion that capacity may lead, not follow population. At the very least, it should induce caution in those states which believe they are building to house future populations that are going to have to be put somewhere. For many states, a decision to have more space is, as the left has been arguing without evidence for some time, a decision to have more prisoners.

This issue is central to our misgivings about federal construction initiatives. Under the major piece of legislation pending in the Congress at this writing, some $6 billion would be provided by Washington according to a formula based on the individual state's general population, the volume of activity of its criminal justice system, and its statewide criminal justice expenditure. However, the populous, high-activity states are not uniformly those with the most overcrowded prisons. Thus, the bill would have quite differential effects around the country. Some populous states with low crowding levels would get federal money to expand capacity and further increase the number of inmates. Some less-populous, low-activity states with high crowding levels would get relatively less money and be less able to improve conditions even if they wanted to. While the bill does provide that each state have a comprehensive plan that "will incorporate innovation and advanced techniques in the design of such facilities," and that personnel and programs will "reflect advanced practices," it will be easy for hastily conceived but well-intentioned applications to go wrong. We are hardly trying to discourage humane and necessary federal initiatives in an area where state governments are lagging badly. But policymakers should be wary of schemes that move blithely from today's superficial numbers game to construction policies with very long-lasting effects. One way to prevent this is to insist on approaching the problem the way it appears in the real world: to judge conditions in each state by some general standard such as the one described above, but without trying to devise a short-cut formula that covers the entire nation.

This chapter has suggested that problems of imprisonment run deeper than any single index or formula and that the problems are not uniformly apportioned among states. The physical measure of capacity used here touches only the surface of the mass of issues which contribute to the total conditions of confinement. Professional corrections associations have enumerated hundreds of standards to which institutions are to adhere. The only thorough approach to improving existing deficiencies is to measure requirements against such a list of uniform standards and to allocate resources first to those systems where they will achieve the most rapid improvement of substandard conditions. As is the case with any allocation rule, some recipients stand to gain more than others under such a formula. States already making a serious effort to comply with standards lose funds under such an approach, in order to benefit those whose prison conditions have been worse. There may be no way to be fair to both states and inmates. If so, only an allocation formula which chooses one or the other makes sense; attempts to blend will achieve neither objective.

Conclusions

For those trying to reach an imprisonment policy directly from quantitative measures, Ogden Nash had the answer: You can't get there from here. The numbers do not speak for themselves, and the facts do not lead inexorably anywhere at all. Normative judgments cannot be avoided, and we conclude this chapter with some of our own.

First, without indicating a clear policy direction, the numbers do go a long way to confirming the bias of the contemporary prison's most severe critics. The measurable aspects of prison life go well beyond the severity of punishments imposed by sentencing courts. The quantitative data simply confirm the fear that the system is imposing additional punishments that range from inhumane to illegally cruel.

Second, the numbers on costs (presented in detail in *American Prisons and Jails*) give increased urgency to the view that for economic reasons alone imprisonment must be considered a scarce resource. This interpretation is unpopular with most conservatives, who feel that America must be willing to "pay any price, bear any burden" in the service of law and order. But a host of studies have caused doubt (to put it mildly) that the current allocation of imprisonment is rationally, let alone optimally, related to either law or order. In Chapter 5, we suggest a plan where some semblance of principle can be induced in the system without imposing excessive financial burdens on it.

Third, the data suggest that at least some of the solutions prescribed by political liberals do not really function as solutions at all. A frequent cry is for the development of alternatives to incarceration, under the presumption that while everyone agrees that some prisoners don't belong there, there is nothing else to do with them. The most widespread of these intended alternatives is probation, introduced at the close of the nineteenth century. There is, however, a real danger that an alternative to prison becomes instead (or also) an alternative to "go thy way and sin no more." In retrospect it is not surprising that, when a third sentencing option was interposed between two others, it was equally likely to draw marginal defendants from both sides, increasing the total number of persons under some sort of sanction. For example, when one compares imprisonment rates with probation rates, no inverse relationship between their use is apparent. Indeed, when jail incarceration rates are also taken into account, what emerges is that rather than high imprisonment/jail incarceration rates being a corollary of low probation rates, there is a positive correlation between the two; and that many of those states which most frequently employ penal confinement to deal with offenders also tend most frequently to employ probation. Table 2.4 shows imprisonment rates (1976), probation rates (1976), and jail incarceration rates (1972) for the twelve states which most frequently use imprisonment and the rates for the twelve which least frequently use it.

Table 2.4

Imprisonment, Probation, and Jail Incarceration Rates for the Twelve States with Highest and Twelve with Lowest Imprisonment Rates

States	Imprisonment Rates (1976)	Probation Rate (1976)	Jail Incarceration Rate (1972)
	Top 12		
District of Columbia	334	904	564
South Carolina	230	826	91
Georgia	225	636	132
North Carolina	214	804	47
Florida	211	513	112
Maryland	192	879	55
Texas	167	860	84
Nevada	159	710	125
Michigan	137	684	46
Oklahoma	133	415	69
Virginia	126	336	66
Arizona	125	590	90
	Bottom 12		
North Dakota	26	331	20
New Hampshire	30	438	37
Minnesota	39	374	15
Hawaii	41	478	28
Massachusetts	46	1,265	32
Rhode Island	53	458	
Pennsylvania	56	521	53
Maine	57	261	24
Utah	60	533	42
Connecticut	62	520	
Alaska	63	465	27
Vermont	66	686	1

SOURCE: U.S. Department of Justice, Law Enforcement Assistance Administration, *Prisoners in State and Federal Institutions on December 31, 1976* (Washington, D.C.: Government Printing Office, 1978).

What liberals too often overlook is that the greater use of one method of punishment does not necessarily imply less frequent use of another. An army that is equipped with a new offensive weapon does not instantly jettison, or limit the use of, all those weapons previously employed. The new weapon is seen as providing extra firepower and as increasingly lethal potential; more of the enemy can be killed. In what some insist on calling the war against crime, the case is not very different. It is a matter of common experience that, to the dismay of penal reformers, courts provided with a new method of punishment designed as an alternative to imprisonment will not infrequently employ it as a means of dealing, not with offenders who might previously have been regarded as candidates for imprisonment but rather with those who might in the past have been accorded more lenient treatment or possibly have escaped any treatment at all.

Moreover, at the lower level of seriousness in the scale of criminality, the supply of candidates for treatment is almost inexhaustible. Additions to the penal armory make it possible therefore to "kill" more offenders, and the body count can be stepped up. Lerman emphasized this in his early study of alternatives to incarceration in California, and now data are available to confirm a national pattern. Liberals who push so hard for nonincarcerative sentencing programs may (here as elsewhere) be serving poorly the interests of those they claim to protect.

The growth of both imprisonment and the social control imposed by alternative forms of sanctions has been argued to be part of the system's response to "what the public wants." Attempting to speak for "the" public has always been an uncertain business at best. Quantitative knowledge of public opinion in most fields is extremely shallow. Sample surveys are necessarily limited to interviews of a few minutes duration, in which it is practically impossible to explore deeply held views. Our knowledge of public opinion about breakfast food is far deeper than knowledge of public opinion about criminal justice. In particular, the survey results available so far are responses to single statements considered in isolation, both from other possibly conflicting claims and from reality. In 1968, when prisons held about 200,000 inmates, 63 percent of the public said that courts did not deal harshly enough with criminals. A decade later, the number of prisoners was nearly 50 percent higher, and 88 percent of respondents said the courts were not harsh enough. Whatever those two samples of the public were responding to, it appears not to have been the actual harshness of sentences meted out. It is relatively difficult even for criminologists to find out just how harsh the courts have been, and therefore hardly surprising that the public view of sanctioning is unrealistic.

There is, however, a deeper problem in guiding incarceration policy by the lights of public opinion. Even when all preferences are perfectly known, it may be impossible to devise a voting system which provides a consistent reflection of these preferences. The preferences may conflict in irreconcilable ways. A recent survey for the National Center for State Courts, for example, found that only 11 percent of respondents supported the notion that judges be required to give the same sentence for a particular crime, regardless of the circumstances of the case (28% supported "a great deal" of power for judges to vary sentences, and 54% supported "limited power"). The difficulty of drawing policy inferences out of popular opinion is suggested, however, by the fact that the same survey showed that 44 percent of the respondents had strong or moderate support for the suggestion that "legislatures should set exact sentences for particular crimes." Vox populi does not always enunciate clearly.

3 Two Patterns of Choice

A major theme of this book is that penal practices, rather than being governed by mysterious and mechanical forces, can be affected by doctrine and conscious policy. That this should require emphasis is itself remarkable. But theorists, at least since Rusche and Kirchheimer in 1939,[1] have argued that the power of doctrine over reality is "imaginary," and today many still regard economics and demography as the primary determinants of the future of imprisonment. Chapter 2 suggested that there are major problems with any approach which, in explaining shifts in the use of imprisonment, relies too heavily on commonsense quantitative indicators such as the baby boom or the crime rate. This chapter elaborates the argument that such determinism misses an important and sometimes crucial explanatory element. Two patterns of development, in America and England, respectively, can be distinguished. They show that although external influences are necessary for any comprehensive understanding of penal development, the discussion cannot begin and end there. Traditional, internal influences, especially beliefs about the purposes and possibilities of the system, must be considered as well.

In dissenting from inevitabilist views of others, we do not claim that any alternative theory of comparable sweep has been presented here. Indeed, we doubt that such an explanatory theory is currently possible, since so many of the links in the process of institutional change are so poorly understood. Our aim is simply to offset the fatalism which has overtaken contemporary policymakers, who see correctional patterns as driven inexorably by factors external to the criminal justice system. To achieve our aim, we need show only that ideas and doctrines can sometimes make a difference. It is well beyond the scope of our effort to construct a social history which catalogues and integrates the broader influences on British and American correctional practice.

A cursory comparison might suggest that the two nations have followed similar paths from the eighteenth century to the present. Certainly today, congestion in prisons is not confined to America. England is also facing what has been called a "crisis of penological resources." The prison population in England and Wales in 1980 stood at a record figure of 44,000, an increase of nearly 370 percent over some 9,400 at the beginning of World War II. The majority of prisoners are held in forty-two prisons built before 1900 and four more built before 1939; less than a quarter of current prison accommodation has been built for twentieth-century need. Some 16,000 prisoners are accommodated two or three to a cell in cells built for single occupancy.[2]

In 1975 Mr. Jenkins, then Home Secretary, stated that a population of 42,000 would place the prison system in a state of crisis.[3] Since that year it has not fallen below that level. Early in 1980 the *Times* named as "the most serious problem facing the prison system . . . appalling overcrowding and a continuing deterioration in conditions."[4] And the chairman of the all-party Parliamentary penal affairs group called on the Home Secretary to deal with "the real issue in prisons, that of numbers" by reducing "the sentence of every prisoner, except those serving life sentences, by half."[5]

Despite these similarities, the British and American institutions of imprisonment have not moved in parallel routes all the way. Shifts in the use of incarceration have been more frequent in Britain than in the United States and have brought the British to their current difficulties by a quite different route from that of the Americans. A comparison of the two histories yields some interesting lessons for both; but since our principal interest is in the American case, we shall use the British experience primarily as a foil. This chapter describes the two general patterns: the American commitment to building and filling prisons remains basically steady over two hundred years, while the British case shows abrupt changes in the mixture of penal sanctions and the rates at which prisons are constructed and offenders are locked up. Then, in the following chapter, we offer a hypothesis to explain the American pattern of past choices and suggest the difficulties in breaking its grip on contemporary policymakers.

Construction Theme and Variations

The standard account of corrections in the United States is Blake McKelvey's *American Prisons*. Its original subtitle was "A Study of American Social History Prior to 1915," and a recent revision changes that to "A History of Good Intentions." In our view, a more appropriate subtitle would be "A History of Overcrowding"; for to a remarkable extent it is an almost numbing chronicle of crowded institutions, building programs designed to relieve the crowding, and more crowding. This cycle, demonstrated in Chapter 2 at the national level for the period since 1955, has dominated America's correctional history. Fortunately, we can let the reader off with a light sentence and subject him to only a brief summary of the story covered in painful detail elsewhere.

The pattern in postrevolutionary Pennsylvania epitomizes the experience of the rest of the states. In 1786, a new penal code substituted sentences of punishment at hard labor for capital punishment in all but two major crimes. In the first applications of this doctrine, local sheriffs sent gangs of convicts out to work on the public roads and the city streets. Bound by chains to each other or to heavy cannon balls, the criminals were dressed in brightly colored pantaloons to show their identity. This novelty, however, provided "a spectacle disturbing to many sober citizens."[6] To many Quakers, and especially to those in the newly constituted Philadelphia Society for Alleviating the Miseries of Public Prisons, this seemed a reversion to the ritual corporal punishments of their former British masters. They persuaded the legislature that a different solution was preferable and that "solitary confinement to hard labor and a total abstinence from spiritous liquors will prove the means of reforming these unhappy creatures."[7] The Walnut Street Jail, later labeled for posterity as the cradle of the penitentiary, was designated as a temporary state prison to house convicts from throughout the state until other provisions could be made.

During the mid-1770s, Philadelphia's leading architect had designed Walnut Street to serve as both jail and house of correction. It was prompted in part by public outrage at the crowded and unsanitary conditions provided for those detained as debtors or awaiting trial. The new doctrine, however, made the existing structure inadequate; and in 1790 a cellblock with interior cells was constructed on the two upper floors to allow separate confinement for those sentenced to "solitary imprisonment." Built on the model of the 1784 Norfolk prison in England, along the lines suggested by the British reformer John Howard, Walnut Street was a real innovation in the United States. A member of the Philadelphia Society, Caleb Lownes, was appointed inspector; he introduced a program of handicrafts, claimed great successes in reforming malefactors, and became a local celebrity. Thus the denouement of McKelvey's story comes somewhat unexpectedly:

> Under the able direction of Caleb Lownes, the Walnut Street jail prospered and attracted wide attention.... His *Account of the Alteration and Present State of the Penal Laws of Pennsylvania* ... stimulated legislators in other states to reform their criminal codes. News of the success of the penitentiary house, where convicts were confined in separate cells at night and re-

leased to work in the courtyard or shops during the day, attracted a stream of visitors. Members of the Philadelphia Society and delegations from other states and abroad were eager to study its program. The attention helped to maintain a state of excitement, and the friendly interviews by dedicated Quakers with the few inmates sentenced to solitary confinement helped to maintain inmate morale. Unfortunately, a flood of commitments soon overcrowded the cellhouse and other accommodations and so disrupted the work program that Caleb Lownes resigned in disgust in 1801.[8]

Under other circumstances, this happy story with the abruptly unhappy ending might be read with some amusement by contemporary readers. If we did not know that this pattern—innovation, enthusiasm, claims of remarkable success followed by disillusion and failure—constitutes America's penal history, McKelvey's punch line without a transition might make a different impression. As it is, Lownes's experience, a passage from new and successful institution to disruption and "disgust" within a few years, has the ring of both truth and familiarity.

As Orlando Lewis wrote later, "The Walnut Street Prison became of nationwide significance not because of any extraordinary conception in its development, but because, for lack of any other model, it became the pattern upon which numerous other State prisons were built and administered.... What was done at Walnut Street conditioned practically absolutely the prison system, so far as there was a system, in the United States for nearly forty years."[9] Inspectors and administrators repeated Lownes's experience in all the states that had followed the fashion of correctional construction. In New York, New Jersey, Massachusetts, Maryland, and Vermont, and soon in Kentucky, Ohio, and New Hampshire, the rhetoric of penal reform was accompanied by the relentless pressure of inmate populations building up in inadequate accommodation. "Serious overcrowding and the consequent disruption of industry and discipline," says McKelvey, "rapidly converted all these prisons into notorious dens of iniquity and roused a wave of popular indignation that in turn prepared the way for a new era of prison reform."[10]

As we shall see, the new era of prison reform in practice meant the development of the penitentiary system, beginning after 1815 in New York and Pennsylvania and spreading throughout America in the next forty years. However, the successive generations of construction provided at best temporary relief from what McKelvey, in an unfortunate metaphor, calls "the incessant lash of increasing convict populations."[11] For example, in the late 1830s, Indiana and Illinois, which had until then managed with jail-like structures, commissioned contractors to build new prisons in Jeffersonville and Alton, respectively. Histories show that the building programs proved to be entirely inadequate: "The 180 cells available at Jeffersonville in 1855 were crowded with 280 convicts, and the 160 cells completed a few years later failed to satisfy the needs of the expanded population. The first 88 cells at Alton in 1845 were already insufficient, and a decade later 300 prisoners were crowding 188 small cells."[12]

There emerged a general pattern of housing two or three prisoners in cells designed for one, and at the time of the outbreak of the Civil War there was only one region (the Northeast) where it was possible to provide prisoners with separate cells. In many states the governor's power to pardon was routinely used to relieve overcrowding, a practice attacked by nineteenth-century penologists as undermining the discipline of many institutions. The end of the Civil War only found matters worse. "The major concern of the era," writes McKelvey as if this were a novelty, "was the housing problem." He continues, "At no time during the second half of the century did the prisons suffer so persistently from serious overcrowding as during the ten years after 1868."[13] This is a significant qualification only if one emphasizes the difference between persistent overcrowding, which characterized this particular decade, and cyclic overcrowding, which characterized most of the states for most of their history. The historian's summary noted that "everywhere expansion occurred." It is worth noting, however, that even after the massive building programs of the seventies and eighties virtually every state had facilities which housed more inmates than the designers had intended. In many places, conditions routinely fell below even the normally low standards. For example, the Missouri prison at Jefferson City, said to be "the most wretched prison in the country,"[14] held 1,200 convicts in 500 cells in 1880 and was to accommodate (if that is the term) 2,300 in the same cells by 1897.

This pressure on correctional capacity, unrelieved except temporarily by a great deal of construction, was the clear result of a widening use of incarceration by American authorities at all levels. Although data from the nineteenth century are incomplete, the official measures of the incarcerated population as a fraction of the total population show a steep, steady rise. The combined jail, prison, and house of correction total climbed from 29 per 100,000 citizens in 1850, to 61 in 1860, 85 in 1870, and 117 in 1880. Thus despite massive administrative difficulties that might have undone a less hardy institution, American imprisonment had survived and flourished in its first hundred years. Neither its demonstrated inability to match capacity to population nor the intermittent theoretical skirmishes surrounding its aims (examined below) had weakened its command of the American penal terrain.

The British Counterpoint

In the century after the American Revolution, the British experience with prison construction was quite different from that of the American. A summary of early developments shows a pattern of fitful, half-hearted efforts to provide the facilities to implement the ideals of Howard and other reformers. Moreover, the early British reluctance to build lasting structures can be seen, at least in part, as a skepticism about the more ambitious penal theories which those reformers had advanced.

Before 1776, about 1,000 criminals annually were being disposed of by transportation from England to her colonies. When this export of convicts ceased, the justices of the peace, who were responsible for local gaols, totally failed to comply with the request of Parliament that the gaols should be enlarged to accommodate such a number. It was in order to meet this contingency that in 1778 a bill, drafted by Blackstone and Eden, was introduced into the House of Commons. The bill provided for the erection of "two plain, strong and substantial edifices or houses which shall be called The Penitentiary Houses."[15] The two penitentiaries were not built, however, partly because the government obtained power to confine convicts in old vessels or "hulks." This expedient also was used to justify a decade of delay, until it was decided to transport convicts to the continent of Australia, a practice which began in 1788. In fact, the temporary floating prisons were to remain in use until the 1850s.

For almost forty years after the American War, prison construction in England consisted of a handful of small facilities built by individual counties. It was not until 1812 that the national government set about building "an immense Penitentiary Prison" to accommodate 1,200 convicts in separate cells. The General Penitentiary of Millbank London took nine years to build and has been called the first example in England of "the modern conception of a prison."[16] But almost from its opening, this was an institution in trouble. "At first," according to an Edwardian historian, "it was very much a plaything for Society, and often visited from the outside; the prisoners were well treated," and the construction of the buildings was designed to implement the fashion for reform through solitude and separation. "But the place soon lost its novelty," Ives goes on, "and soon lapsed into the hands of a regular committee and the salaried officials."[17] In these hands (of what would today be called correctional administrators), there was produced "that long record of dreary cruelties and bungling experiments which for a good many years were carried out at Millbank": suicides, riots, and a serious epidemic of "a somewhat peculiar character" which was probably typhus and which forced the complete abandonment of the entire building for almost a year. In the late 1830s Millbank was the object of furious attacks in the House of Lords, in one case for keeping three girls less than ten years of age in solitary confinement for over a year. Whether the various charges were correct in their particulars, Ives wrote in summary, "the admitted facts are bad enough."[18]

During this period, humanitarian complaints were not the only ones leveled against the British use of incarceration. In comparison with other traditional punishments, imprisonment had defects which were not shared by its historical precursors. First, both the death penalty and transportation were relatively cheap, whereas the new penitentiaries were extremely expensive. Indeed, Millbank was later described by the Webbs as "one of the most costly buildings that the world had then seen since the pyramids of Egypt."[19] Second, the traditional punishments were longer lasting: capital punishment was final for all, and only 5 percent of the convicts sent to Australia ever did return to the United Kingdom.[20] Only imprisonment for life carried out literally could achieve the same object. But, quite apart from the criminal law and the public conscience, the prohibitive expense of imprisoning offenders sine die would not permit it except for the most serious and persistent cases. And this meant that prisons had to deal with their own failures. The problem of recidivism did not arise in relation to the death penalty, and in the case of transportation it was exported. As long as it was possible to pursue, in America and Australia, the policy that Benjamin Franklin described as "emptying their jails into our settlements,"[21] there was no need for Britain to worry about what offenders did in the future.

In the first four decades of the nineteenth century, then, the British actually built few prisons and apparently considered imprisonment an adjunct of transportation. At the latter's peak in the 1830s an annual average of 5,000 persons were transported, and the prison capacity could not possibly absorb them. Indeed, according to Wines, "The necessity for building prisons in England would have been avoided [altogether] if the people, first of the United States and then of Australia, had not absolutely refused to allow the deportation of convicted felons to those countries."[22] Thus during the era of highest American enthusiasm for the institution of imprisonment— the 1820s and 1830s—the prison had not captured the British imagination to nearly the same extent. The British had experienced 1776 as a watershed, but one yielding quite different results. First with the hulks and then with a renewed commitment to transportation (163,000 offenders transported between 1788 and 1868), the British met their needs without initially giving imprisonment a central place. Moreover, they began by reserving incarceration for minor property

offenders, whereas the Americans were using it "across the board."
The significance of these differences was to appear as the nineteenth
century unwound.

Toward the middle of the nineteenth century, the institution of
transportation came increasingly under attack. As Australia developed and prospered it came to resent the influx of felons, while to
many Britons transportation to a prosperous colony seemed insufficiently severe. A wave of prison construction followed, intended
to house offenders who previously would have been transported.
Within six years after the penitentiary at Pentonville opened in 1842,
fifty-four new prisons were built based on that model. By the formal
end of transportation in 1868, some 27,000 offenders were confined in
convict and local prisons. And over the next ten years, the inmate
population continued to climb; by 1878 the British incarceration rate
actually was higher than the American. The combined prison and jail
population in England was 118 inmates for every 100,000 in the general population, whereas the comparable figure (i.e., not including·
the houses of correction) for the United States was slightly less than
100.

At a superficial level, then, the British and American institutions of
imprisonment might seem to have emerged from their first century
with a similar place in their respective societies. The British had
exceeded the Americans in their total incarceration rate, and in 1878
had turned the administration of all prisons over to the national government. Yet, in our view, the two patterns were quite different. Very
short stays in local facilities made up a much larger fraction of the
British total. And even for that smaller fraction of more serious offenders, the British pattern can be distinguished from the American.
This is clear if we go beyond the chronicles of correctional construction and look to the respective purposes which the British and Americans thought were being served.

The tendency to get criminals "out of sight," writes Max Grunhut,
"goes back to a primitive stage of criminal law."[23] In his erudite, if
eccentric, investigation of "the paleontology of penal law," Hans von
Hentig begins his account of the evolution of punishment by noting
that society's most primitive form of self-defense is expulsion from
the community. At a later stage in history, when abandonment to
nature no longer meant certain death, other methods of punishment
were developed, among ·them capital punishment and deportation,
which was often "a bloodless form of capital punishment."[24] The
early British attitude to imprisonment was very much in this tradition. "General opinion," writes Lionel Fox, "still inclined to the simple view that the best thing to do with convicted felons was to get rid
of them, one way or another, and forget about them."[25] Even Ben-

tham, who is generally regarded as an enthusiastic advocate of imprisonment, recognized the force of this general opinion in political events. He had spoken of transportation's appeal with some irony: "I rid myself of the sight of you: the ship that bears you away saves me from witnessing your sufferings—I shall give myself no more trouble about you."[26]

Considered in this light, the British attitude to imprisonment is at least in emphasis different from the American. Howard's idealist theories notwithstanding, for the first fifty years of the institution, British practices and construction policies seem to reflect a search for alternative ways of disposing of offenders rather than a belief in a beneficent social institution. Of course, we do not deny that reform later had its vogue in nineteenth-century Britain penology. Sober citizens came to visit Pentonville and learn its lessons of moral order just as they visited Cherry Hill in Pennsylvania. The desire to banish criminals may have dominated, but it did not exhaust the justifying purposes of the early British prison. Even so, this reformatory impulse was complex, and its influence on doctrine and popular hopes for the institution appears different in the two countries. The two strands of what would today be called the rehabilitative ideal are exemplified by the writings and actions of two men, John Howard and Jeremy Bentham.

Michael Ignatieff has summarized nicely the distinct doctrinal paths taken by the two great British reformers. "Howard and Bentham," Ignatieff says, "both denied criminal incorrigibility, but from diametrically opposed positions—one accepting the idea of original sin, the other denying it. One insisted on the universality of guilt, the other on the universality of reason. Materialists like Bentham and Priestley asserted that men could be improved by correctly socializing their instincts for pleasure. Howard believed men could be changed by awakening their consciousness of sin." Thus although the early prison is sometimes seen as a purely rationalist and Enlightenment institution, such a view ignores another powerful influence on it, for "Howard's thought was cast not in the vernacular of mechanism, but in an older religious language." The two influences were mutually reinforcing; as Ignatieff shows, by collapsing the mind-body distinction "the materialist psychology offered an apparently scientific explanation for Howard's claim that men's moral behavior could be altered by disciplining their bodies."[27]

Although these two strands were intertwined, they seem to have had differing effects on the British and American penal traditions. By "traditions" we refer not to the daily routine of particular prisons but to the rhetoric and mythology which have such great influence on any social institution. There is no claim here that in 1821 Auburn in New

York was a nicer place to be than Millbank in England. Rather, we suggest that, from the beginning, the complex reformatory spirit described by Ignatieff left a different emphasis in the respective countries: in England, the secular rationalism of Bentham, who sought in his 1791 Panopticon "a machine for grinding rogues honest";[28] in America, greater hope for the process of convict reformation that would parallel "the spiritual awakening of a believer." Ignatieff has called it a hope that "from out of the silence of an ascetic vigil, the convict and believer alike would begin to hear the inner voice of conscience and feel the transforming power of God's love."[29] He was writing about the general Quaker influence, but the spirit he describes so well had more powerful effects on social attitudes to imprisonment in America than in England. The early emphasis on religious ideals as a basis for correctional reform had a continuing effect on the popular imagination. Such ultimately irrational expectations are hard to change. The rationalist British justifications for imprisonment—the desire to banish and the secular view of the prospects for reform—were to prove easier to revise than their American counterparts.

The relatively modest British expectations can be seen in both the use and justification of imprisonment. In the late eighteenth century, the British prison was not asked to carry nearly the burden of the American institution. Initially, imprisonment in Britain was a middle-range punishment for offenses not serious enough to require capital punishment or transportation. Crimes against the person, and burglary or housebreaking, were still regarded as too serious to have an offender "let off" with only a prison sentence. Later, after penal servitude was substituted for transportation and convicts served their sentences and were released in England, imprisonment played an increased role. But even then, compared with American attitudes, the claims made for the British prison were quite limited. Millbank was considered frankly experimental, and the results were hardly encouraging. Pentonville, opened in 1842, probably represents both in practice and construction the highest hope for the nineteenth-century penitentiary in England. Its solitary cells were designed to produce the kind of reformation for which Howard had hoped. However, as an official inquiry later reported, as early as 1857 "the original intention . . . appears . . . to have been lost sight of" and "the main object of the separate confinement had come to be deterrence."[30] By the 1870s, while the Americans were enthusiastically developing a new theory of the Reformatory and building new facilities to apply it, officials in England were taking quite a different view.

The prison should impose "severe penal discipline," said Sir Edmund du Cane, the first chairman of the Board of Prison Commissioners, but he was not sanguine about the effects of that discipline on the individual subjected to it. "To my mind, there can be no greater fallacy," he wrote, "than the supposition that the greater the proportion of re-convictions the less effective the system of punishment.... Punishment is inflicted much more for the purpose of deterring from crime the enormous number of *possible* criminals than for any effect on the actual criminal himself."[31] In 1878 the national government took over the administration of all prisons, and the dominance of this view became absolute. For twenty years thereafter, according to Fox, British imprisonment "presented the pattern of deterrence by severity of punishment, uniformly, rigidly and efficiently applied. For death itself the system had substituted a living death. It became legendary ... even in Russia."[32] And this dominance of deterrence as a justifying purpose was not something invented by the administrators. Du Cane, Fox shows, was a responsive public servant: "Parliament, the Judges and the public called for such a system, and he provided it: he was even required, so hard was it to satisfy the more convinced exponents of deterrence, to defend it against the charge of exaggerated sentimentality."[33]

Thus although a comparison of total incarceration rates in 1878 might have suggested that imprisonment was as firmly entrenched in England as in the United States, the deeper reality was quite different. In America the penitentiary had simply swept before it the demonstrated failures either to keep up with the demand for prison space or to reduce the crime rate by meeting that demand. New problems were met by new bursts of theorizing and new construction programs. In England, imprisonment had played a variety of parts in the penal gavotte and had offered relatively limited justifications for them. It had started later in a serious way and had been received with relatively less enthusiasm. The British seem never to have caught what Tocqueville was to call the monomanie that dominated nineteenth-century American attitudes to the penitentiary. Against this background, the developments of the second century of the institution may be somewhat less surprising.

Separate Paths to the Present

After about 1878, the British use of incarceration began to decline even more sharply than it had increased in the middle years of the century. By 1900, the incarceration rate had dropped by more than half. Throughout this period and well into the twentieth century many prisons in England were actually closed. By 1894, for example, of the 113 local prisons taken over by the British government, only fifty-six remained open. In that year the total prison population had fallen to

18,000; six years later it had dropped to 17,000, a decline of 45 percent in less than twenty-five years.

In figure 3.1 we have shown the gross shifts in the use of incarceration in the United Kingdom and the United States over the past century. We emphasize the adjective "gross"; especially for the early part of the hundred-year period, the graph must be used for illustrative purposes only. With available data, it is not possible to present a continuous series for the two countries; the series overlap, and in the overlapping portion of the graph they give the possibly incorrect impression that the American jail population was rising substantially faster than the country's prison population. Nonetheless, it is useful to present the material in this way because it dramatizes the point arising from these and all other available data: after about 1878, the British incarceration rate began to drop and the American rate continued to climb.

What accounts for the divergence? At a superficial level, table 3.1 shows the components of the initial policy shift in Britain from 1878 to 1900. It can be seen that in the first five-year period the imprisonment rate was more than half of the indictment rate, whereas in the last five-year period it had fallen to one-third of the indictment rate. Although this table may reflect a change in prosecutorial practice, it is more a description than an explanation. The commonsense view might be that the crime rate had dropped and that, whether as cause or effect of this, incarceration was less necessary than before. This is precisely the claim made by du Cane at the time: prison population was dropping because "our penal reformatory system has been made effective. . . . in that which is the main purpose of all, the repression of crime."[34]

Du Cane's claim was not to go unchallenged. In 1895 an official inquiry by the Gladstone Committee reported that he had been mistaken. It was true, they said, that there had been a small but steady decrease in crime, but it was not at all proportionate to the decline in the number of inmates. Only about one-tenth of the decrease in prison population was due to the decrease in crime; the rest was due to "the diminution in the average length of sentences." Moreover, the recidivism rate, which might be regarded as a better measure of the success of the prison system, had in fact remained "as great as ever." Indeed, they said that "it is difficult . . . to avoid the belief that the proportion of reconvictions during the last 20 years has increased."[35]

Without entering the thicket of the Gladstone Committee's analysis, we can see that they shared with du Cane a belief that incarceration and crime rates are somehow related. We shall consider this commonsense assumption in more detail below; here we simply note how the Gladstone report perpetuates a simplistic view of a

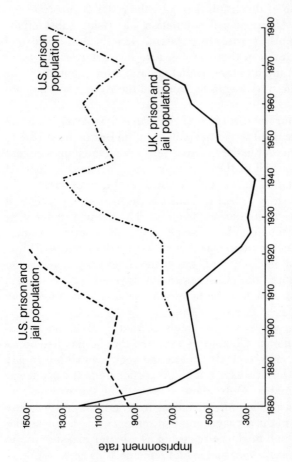

FIGURE 3.1: British and American incarcerated populations, 1880–1980. Source: Derived from U.S. Department of Commerce and Labor, Bureau of the Census, *Prisoners and Juvenile Delinquents in Institutions, 1904* (Washington, D.C.: Government Printing Office, 1907); and ibid., *Prisoners and Juvenile Delinquents in Institutions, 1910* (Washington, D.C.: GPO, 1918); U.S. Department of Commerce, Bureau of the Census, *Number of Prisoners in Penal Institutions, 1917 and 1922* (Washington, D.C.: GPO, 1923): ibid., *Prisoners in State and Federal Prisons and Reformatories, 1926* (Washington, D.C.: GPO, 1927); ibid., *Prisoners in State and Federal Prisons and Reformatories, 1926–38* (Washington, D.C.: GPO, 1939); U.S. Department of Justice, Law Enforcement Assistance Administration, *Sourcebook of Criminal Justice Statistics, 1973 and 1978* (Washington, D.C.: GPO); Great Britain, Central Statistical Office, *Annual Abstract of Statistics*, vols. 1–83 titled *Statistical Abstract for the United Kingdom*; Great Britain, Home Department, *Report of the Commissioners of Prisoners and Directors of Convict Prisons*, for 1904, 1910, 1923, 1926.

complex process. One could, of course, construct a set of theories to explain developments in this way. Consider, for example, the British pattern some years after du Cane's retirement; the period is selected because of data availability. As figure 3.2 shows, from 1900 to 1915, crime and imprisonment are at least moving in the same general direction. Does this mean the prisons had temporarily stopped reforming criminals, or had imprisonment become the dependent variable and been pushed upward by a rising crime rate? According to the latter hypothesis, the period 1908–1915 is an especially good fit; a declining use of imprisonment is made possible by declining levels of crime. After 1916, however, the linkage theorists have to shift gears. The rates are diverging, and the deterrence/incapacitation variant of du Cane's argument now emerges. It could be claimed that the crime rate drops toward 1920 *because* the imprisonment rate went up. But these gyrations are more than slightly strained. In considering the causes of fluctuations in imprisonment rates, it is a mistake to look for the simple billiard ball sequences of physics or mechanics. What one commonly finds is a complex of events and actions which are related synchronously rather than sequentially. The interrelations in the late nineteenth and early twentieth century in England include changes in the law and its procedure, changes in sentencing practice, changes in public attitudes toward criminals, the nationalization of local prisons and the attendant drive for economy, the activities of the newly formed Howard Association, and the views of influential experts who "had come to the conclusion that the government prisons were not conducted in such a manner as to promote the moral elevation of offenders."[36] These help to explain, not by showing a simple causal sequence but by making intelligible the sharp decline in imprisonment rates.

Since our primary interest here is in the role of policymakers, we must excuse ourselves from attempting a comprehensive social history that weighs and integrates the above factors. We want simply to insist that, in all the modern jargon about macroeconomic trends and lead indicators, the so-called soft influences too often get lost. This is especially true of the beliefs of the men who made the actual decisions. We maintain that an understanding of their doctrine at least makes intelligible the late nineteenth-century shift in the British use of incarceration.

The officials of the Victorian period confronted what du Cane's successor called "an uneasy feeling in the public mind" about the British prison system. "This feeling," wrote Ruggles-Brise, "found echo in the Press; not only were the principles of prison treatment as prescribed in the Prisons Acts criticized, but the prison authority itself, and the constitution of that authority, were held to be re-

Table 3.1
British Indictment and Imprisonment Rates (1877–1901)

Period	Average of Yearly Totals Persons Tried for Indictable Offenses	Indictment Rate[a] per 100,000 Population	Daily Average Prison Population	Imprisonment Rate[a] per 100,000 Population
1877–1881	57,233	226	29,695	118
1882–1886	59,259	220	26,566	99
1887–1891	56,280	198	20,740	73
1892–1896	53,863	182	17,340	59
1897–1901	52,567	165	17,492	55

SOURCE: Adapted from G. Rose, *The Struggle for Penal Reform* (Chicago: Quadrangle Books, 1961), appendix 1, pp. 289–90.
[a]Figures rounded to nearest whole number.

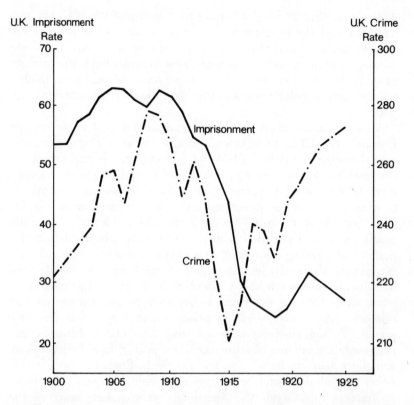

FIGURE 3.2: Crimes and prisoners per 100,000 population United Kingdom (1900–1925). Source: Derived from Great Britain, Home Department, *Criminal Statistics: England and Wales* (annual publ.); and Great Britain, Home Department, *Reports of the Commissioners of Prisons and Directors of Convict Prisons* (annual publ.).

sponsible for many grave evils.... It was impossible for the Government of the day to ignore this fierce indictment."[37] True, leading politicians of the day, like Asquith and Gladstone, were completely disenchanted with the prison system. But governments often survive fierce indictments when there is some bulwark, either bureaucratic or more general, against attack. Why did British officials feel forced to choose a smaller role for imprisonment in the late nineteenth century rather than feel forced to justify its continued extensive role?

In our view, it was in large part for doctrinal reasons that the British officials of the day had far greater freedom to choose imprisonment's future than did their American counterparts. As Fox has said, "The use of imprisonment as a form of punishment in itself... had hardly gained acceptance before it was overtaken by the doubt whether after all it was a very good idea, so that subsequent legislation was devoted rather to abating than developing its use."[38]

As early as 1863 an official inquiry by a House of Lords Committee had undercut the justification that was central to the prison's defenders in the United States. "We do not consider," said the Committee, "that the moral reformation of the offender holds the primary place in the prison system."[39] And as we have shown, by the 1870s a narrow view of deterrence was the institution's main doctrinal support.

After the mid-century period of genuine efforts at implementing Howard's rehabilitative theories, and after the subsiding of the panic over the return on ticket-of-leave of formerly transported criminals, the British were again free to tinker with the prison system by once more reformulating its purposes. The social institution of imprisonment never took hold—never captured people's imagination—in England the way it did in the United States. Its British roots were not nearly as deep. Compared with the Americans, the British in this period had a rather clear-eyed view of the institution. Many already feared that it was only loosely related to crime and its control. Even du Cane, whom we saw above taking credit for a safer England, could admit that "I do not think that either an increase or a decrease in crime is due so exclusively to prison systems as it has been asserted."[40] Ruggles-Brise believed that "the prison administrator plays only a small and obscure executive part"[41] in reducing crime, and there seem to have been few people in England who felt that either the administrator or the prison should, or could, assume a preeminent role. While the Americans were making much of the innovation of the Reformatory, the British felt it "would simply be a prison."[42] Elements inseparable from prison life, in their view, made American hopes sad and misguided. In particular, they saw religious instruction as "coming to something very little indeed,"[43] and prison labor as having no moral value because it was useless and forced.

To suggest that imprisonment became less used because theorists, officials, and interested citizens regarded it with disfavor does not, of course, accord with Rusche and Kirchheimer's analysis of these developments. Their interpretation of the decline in the use of imprisonment in England in the last quarter of the nineteenth century is simply that "the immense expansion of industrial production ... provided for a maximum absorption of labor power. The senseless imprisonment of individuals became undesirable and out of step with the times."[44] Yet this account, in which economic conditions drive penal policy, is not particularly plausible. The industrial revolution in Britain had essentially been completed by mid-century, and the country's economic preeminence and superiority in the world market was absolute. For the working classes the worst was over; as Rusche and Kirchheimer themselves point out, it was earlier, between 1780 and 1830, that "the height of pauperism was reached." From then on conditions began to improve, and by 1850 Britain was solidly established as the world's greatest industrial power. The immense expansion of industrial production and of employment had long been underway by 1878; yet in that year the number of prisoners was "absolutely at its maximum in the whole history of the nation."[45] The commonsense link of poverty levels and imprisonment rates does not survive the British experience of the latter part of the nineteenth century.

In figure 3.1 the stages can be traced of the divergence between American and British practice. After dropping through the 1880s, the British incarceration rate stabilized around sixty-three per 100,000 (in 1905). The decade following this plateau brought a reduction in the use of imprisonment by more than half. Where 21,000 inmates had been confined in 1905, only 9,000 were held in 1919. At this point the incarceration rate was 24.6 per 100,000, less than half that of the turn of the century and about one-fifth of the 118 per 100,000 peak recorded in 1880. It is true that there had been a decline in the crime rate over those years, from 278 to 247 per 100,000 population, but this represents only an 11 percent increase, which is disproportionately small compared to the fall in the imprisonment rate.

For the first quarter of the twentieth century national prison statistics for America are not available on an annual basis. However, independent enumerations of prisoners were made in 1904, 1910, and 1923, and annual data became available beginning in 1926. It is possible, therefore, to compare imprisonment rates for America and Britain in those years. It must be remembered, however, that the British figures include all those who would have been incarcerated as jail inmates in America, while jail populations are not included in the American figures. In other words, the American figures consistently underrate the extent to which incarceration was employed. The respective rates are shown in table 3.2.

An intensification of the doctrinal trend discussed above underlies the renewed decline in British incarceration rates after 1910. The disenchantment with imprisonment, Fox writes, led to "a remarkable series of statutes seeking to keep out of prison large classes of offenders for whom imprisonment is neither suitable nor necessary, and to provide better ways of dealing with them."[46] These statutes included the Probation of Offenders Act of 1907, the first genuine probation statute in England; the Children's Act of 1908, which prohibited the imprisonment of children under fourteen and restricted its use for those between fourteen and sixteen; the Prevention of Crime Act of 1908, which sought to remove from prison people under twenty-one; the Mental Deficiency Act of 1913, which kept out or

Table 3.2
Imprisonment Rates per 100,000 Population

Year	United States	England and Wales
1904	69	62
1910	75	62
1923	74	31
1926 (1/1/26)	80	28

SOURCE: U.S. Department of Commerce, Bureau of the Census, *Prisoners in State and Federal Prisons and Reformatories, 1926* (Washington, D.C.: Government Printing Office, 1927); and Great Britain Home Department, *Reports of the Commissioners of Prisons and Directors of Convict Prisons* (1904, 1910, 1923, 1926).
NOTE: The figures for the United States in this table are not continuous with the series above because the earlier figures, as noted there, included unsentenced prisoners and prisoners in jails, city prisons, etc. The 1904 figures do not include persons imprisoned for nonpayment of fine. Figures rounded to the nearest whole number.

removed mental defectives from prison; and, finally, the Criminal Justice Act of 1914, which required magistrates to allow time for the payment of fines unless there were good reasons for not doing so. Of all the statutes, that which had by far the greatest impact on prison population was the last, for the number of persons sent to prison in default of payment of fines fell from 50,000 in 1910 to 15,000 in 1921.

At least in the early part of this period judges appeared to respond to the rigors of incarceration by further shortening sentences. Sir Alfred Wills, a British judge writing in 1895, said, "The iron severity and rigidity of our convict prisons is one of the things that makes most of us—myself certainly—shrink from the long sentences that are really the only things of any use."[47] The implication appears to be that long prison sentences might have been imposed if the prison regime had been less harsh. But penal reformers in England were less concerned with improving prisons than with emptying them. Bernard Shaw wrote, "Imprisonment as it exists today, . . . is a worse crime than any of those committed by its victims."[48] The Webbs charged that "it passes the wit of man to contrive a prison which shall not be gravely injurious to the minds of the vast majority of the prisoners, if not also of their bodies. So far as can be seen at present, the most hopeful of 'prison reforms' is to keep people out of prison altogether."[49] Moreover, these sentiments influenced policy and practice, even to the extent of receiving official echoes: "We record our opinion," wrote the Commissioners of Prisons in 1922, "that the best way to effect real economies is to bring about a substantial reduction in the number of persons committed to prison."[50]

We emphasize the difference between the foregoing analysis and a comprehensive social history that integrates the various influences on incarceration rates over time. As noted above, we have left it to expert social historians to set the determinative attitudes to the prison in a larger intellectual and political context. Ignatieff, for example, sees a link between the Quakers' criminal justice views and their persecution in England for religious nonconformism. Starting with a desire to limit the state's right to dictate conscience, they were led to campaigns against capital punishment and for penal reform. In this view, the powerful Quaker influence on penology in both England and America "followed from their doctrinal concern to set strict limits to the use of state force."[51] This kind of argument, while interesting and persuasive, is not essential to our more modest claim. We have tried only to show that, whatever its broader setting, "doctrinal concern" played a significant part in the various shifts in the use of imprisonment in Britain. Our purpose has been, by analogy, to convince contemporary policymakers that they can do more than respond to a demand for prison space created by forces over which they have no control.

What were the American views that led this country to extend further its use of incarceration after the 1870s? David Rothman suggests two reasons why, in the post–Civil War decades, penal reformers in America believed "the appropriate task was to reform incarceration, not to launch a fundamental attack upon it."[52] First, they reasoned that the abolition of prison would lead to the restoration of colonial penal practices, such as the gallows, whipping posts, and edicts of banishment. Second, they were committed to the idea that prisons could accomplish rehabilitation. "The prospect of doing good, not merely the desire to avoid greater harm, ultimately bound another generation of well-meaning observers to the practice of incarceration."[53] In the following chapter, we shall pursue this question and try to integrate it into a broader view of the solidity of the American institution of imprisonment. For the moment, it is enough to agree with Rothman that neither in the general public nor in the specialized community was there anything comparable to the storm around du Cane's last years in office. By 1900, although the Progressives were devising new adjuncts to it in probation and parole, the American prison stood securely at the center of the nation's criminal justice system. Faced with "glaring institutional abuse" the Americans simply "came up with a new design"[54] in the form of a new theory of the Reformatory and a successful effort to find money to build it. They were undaunted by the British opinion that their scheme was "in many respects . . . fanciful and extravagant"[55] and that it showed once again "that excessive zeal for aiming at the moral or religious reform of prisoners."[56]

After the turn of the century, a few American specialists used the British example to support misgivings about the prison. Edwin

Sutherland, the distinguished criminologist, wrote in 1934 in "The Decreasing Prison Population of England":

> Prisons are being demolished and sold in England because the supply of prisoners is not large enough to fill them. The number of prisoners in custody in England in 1930 was less than half the number in 1857, though the population of England was twice as large. This decrease was not a direct result of a reduction in the general crime rate, but rather of changes in penal policies. An analysis of the reasons for this decrease should be useful in the attempts to revise the penal policies of the United States, where the prison population has been increasing and where overcrowding of prisons is a chronic evil even though many huge prisons have been constructed.[57]

In general, however, even reformers in the United States did not share Sutherland's view. Thomas Mott Osborne, for example, hailed by Franklin Roosevelt as "the great pioneer" of penal reform in the century, seems not to have been concerned about the size of inmate populations. Indeed, he spoke with some pride of "the hordes of miscellaneous humanity at Auburn and Sing Sing struggling along with their problem of making a self-governing democracy work."[58] He accepted the American social institution as it existed and sought to achieve change within the system. It is characteristic of his attitude that, so far from attacking the penitentiary system, it was precisely those "large maximum security institutions . . . with populations of convicts of all stripes and brands," above the gates of which he wanted to have inscribed Abraham Lincoln's words: "As I understand the spirit of our institutions, it is designed to promote the elevation of men."[59]

Osborne's basic faith in the eventual success of the institution was echoed in 1923 by Roscoe Pound, to whom "it [seemed] clear that preventive justice would play a large part in the law of the future." Pound was an enthusiastic supporter of probation and parole as adjuncts to imprisonment, all of which he saw as components in a scientific system of matching cures to diseases. "We worked out a prison system independently, parallel with England," he wrote. "We developed the idea of reformatory institutions and of penal treatment directed toward restoration of the offender to useful citizenship." While Pound saw defects in that system, his response was to overhaul it, not to turn away as did so many of his British contemporaries. In the end, it was this difference between England and the United States to which Pound attributed his optimism: "The prospect here is much more hopeful than at any other point in American criminal justice. We are less in a rut here . . . . Penal treatment is not unlikely to continue to be characteristically the American field of progress in criminal law and administration."[60]

Indeed it was, at least in quantity. From the beginning of the century until Pound wrote these words, the American prison population was growing at a faster rate than the general population. The 57,000 prisoners held in 1904 represented sixty-nine inmates for every 100,000 in the general population. By 1926 the number of inmates had grown by 40,000, reflecting an incarceration rate of eighty per 100,000. In the years following, the increase accelerated perceptibly. By the end of 1939 the incarceration rate was at a peak in excess of 130 per 100,000 population, nearly twice the level of the turn of the century. All this while the British were refining "a tradition . . . that nobody should receive a sentence to prison unless all other sentences are impracticable."[61]

What might all this have to do with crime rates? In our view, not very much. Consider figures 3.3 and 3.4, which display crime and imprisonment rates in the two countries over the past half-century.

Four things emerge most clearly from the graphs. First is the remarkable parallelism between the movement of gross crime rates in the two countries over the last half-century. Second, there is the marked divergence in imprisonment rates—a divergence which is substantially understated in the diagram because of the fact that the American rates do not include, as the British do, jail inmates. It is notable that in 1940, when the British imprisonment rate was at its lowest after declining for nearly a decade, the American rate was at its highest after climbing steadily over the same period, although in neither country was there any corresponding movement in crime rates.

Third, there is the remarkable independence of the movements of the two rates in both countries and the frequency with which they moved in opposite directions. This is particularly marked in America. For the most part, the crime rate moved steadily upward, while the imprisonment rate appears to have heard a different drummer and executed improvisatory leaps and swoops, suddenly rising to a peak at a time when the crime rate was pursuing a level course, and plunging steeply at a time when the crime rate was, equally steeply, climbing. In Britain the crime and imprisonment rates moved more closely together, but here too the congruence is irregular and there is frequent divergence. For example, the downward trend in imprisonment rates in the 1930s took place at a time when crime rates were steadily climbing.

The fourth observation questions the claim of causal connection between falling imprisonment rates and rising crime rates. The examples of this kind of correspondence referred to in the previous paragraph lend no support to any causal inference. Some Americans, for example, might be tempted to infer a causal connection during the 1960s between the fall in imprisonment rates and the corresponding

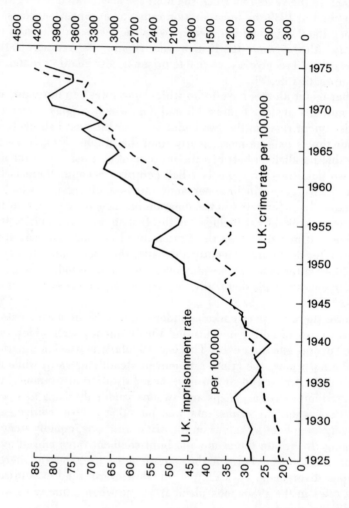

FIGURE 3.3: U.K. imprisonment rate and crime rate per 100,000. Source: Crime rates derived from Great Britain, Central Statistical Office, *Annual Abstract of Statistics*. Imprisonment rates derived from sources in fig. 3.1.

increase in crime rates. But the upward movement in crime began some twenty years before, and continued steadily despite the fact that throughout that twenty years the imprisonment rate was also climbing, albeit less steadily. Moreover, when the imprisonment rate reached its second highest level on record, the crime rate had climbed along with it to an unprecedented level and continued to climb without interruption. The same applies to the British example. From 1933 to 1940 the imprisonment rate fell and the crime rate rose. Again, however, causal inference is rendered implausible because, when the downward trend in the imprisonment rate was reversed and it moved upward for over a decade, this was not reflected in any corresponding change in direction of movement in the crime rate.

An Unexpected Convergence?

Given the doctrinal patterns described above, the developments after the late 1930s are surprising. Indeed, apparently in the same year of 1939, both national imprisonment rates took uncharacteristic turns: The British rate ceased its more or less stable meandering and began an upward swing that has lasted to the present with only brief interruptions. The American rate ceased, albeit temporarily, both its long-term upward trend and its short-term burst of growth since the 1920s. Some commentary on this is required.

The conventional wisdom about the controlling influence of wartime on imprisonment rates does not take us very far. In the United States, the drop in the use of incarceration began fully two years before the country's entry into the War. Would Rusche and Kirchheimer argue for some half-conscious, preemptive liberalization of penal policy to provide soldiers for an American war effort few believed would occur? Also, the British imprisonment rate climbed sharply throughout the entire period of the war. If the time-series data have laid to rest the notion of crime or unemployment as a causal indicator of imprisonment, what more can be said?

We believe a partial explanation can again be found, at least in the British case, in the factor of doctrine. Ironically, after resisting for a hundred years, the British came finally in the 1930s to accept what Ruggles-Brise had called "the radical views on the nature of punishment" of "our kinsmen on the other side of the Atlantic."[62] According to the leading British scholars, when these traditionally American views were applied the British imprisonment rate started to rise. Thus Rupert Cross points to "the baneful influence of the myth that prison could be reformative if only the authorities were given enough time" as the cause of "the vast increase in the average length of sentence which took place between 1938 and 1958."[63] And Fox,

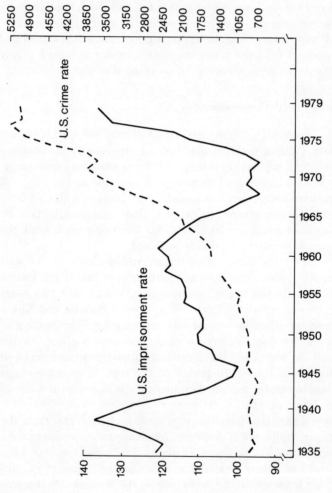

FIGURE 3.4: U.S. imprisonment rate and crime rate. Figures for the United States for 1958 and 1959 are not comparable. The crime rate figures for 1935–57 include incidents of negligent manslaughter. More recent crime rate figures do not. Source: Crime rates derived from U.S. Department of Justice, Federal Bureau of Investigation, *Uniform Crime Reports* (Washington, D.C.: Government Printing Office, 1935–). Imprisonment rates derived from sources in fig. 3.1.

writing as chairman of the English Prison Commission, wrote of "the prison system of 1950" as "the natural growth of the seminal ideas of the years between the wars," the first and most basic of those ideas being that "the prison regime should be one of constructive training, moral, mental and vocational."[64] He pointed out further that "the training that can be given will affect only those who are there long enough to profit by it.... [P]enologists, prison administrators and informed opinion in general," he wrote, had "unsparingly condemned... the short sentence."[65] Thus judges and magistrates were advised to avoid imposing short prison sentences because they would not allow time for rehabilitative techniques to operate successfully. As a result, by 1951 the daily average population of English prisons had reached the highest figure recorded since the records were begun in 1878: 22,500, double the prewar average.

This trend has never been reversed and, although the British imprisonment rate has never reached parity with the American figure, the gap between the two rates in the third quarter of the century narrowed (as shown in fig. 3.4) to a remarkable degree. It is only recently, largely as a result of prison population pressures and negative research reports, that the rehabilitative ideal has been officially questioned, notably in two official documents published in 1977: the report of the Advisory Council on the Penal System, *The Length of Prison Sentences*,[66] and from the Home Office *A Review of Criminal Justice Policy*.[67]

Ideas and Imprisonment

It may be that the "power of doctrine over reality," which some determinists have dismissed as "imaginary,"[68] is not present or not easy to discern in many fields of human activity. But in the sphere of penal practice it is clearly manifest. We have not attempted to describe the mechanisms of this influence, although it is possible to speculate. First, there is little here to interest those who seek or have attained economic or political power. Second, and this is of course directly related to the first point, Sir Samuel Romilly exaggerated only slightly when he told Jeremy Bentham that the general public "does not care tuppence for prisons and prisoners at any time."[69] This creates a power vacuum in which the ideas of those who are interested may exert an influence out of all proportion to their numbers. The effect, in our view, should be to encourage those who (whatever their ideology) do care and do have ideas.

At a minimum, a historical comparison of England and America induces caution about general theories which purport to predict the future of imprisonment by the use of general economic trends or specific lead indicators. Over time, many commonsense causal or associative links simply fall apart. An awareness of the role of doctrine can at least be a supplement and a corrective. Whatever one may believe ultimately drives such doctrinal choices, their proximate influence seems clear in the contrast described above. More centralized in its organization and less deeply rooted in the political culture, British imprisonment responded to doctrinal shifts by sharply expanding and contracting its role in society.

Some may be tempted to say that the British were forced by circumstance to adopt a pragmatic attitude to the prison. This argument would maintain that the persistence of the hulks, of transportation, and of capital punishment (albeit much reduced in scope) for much of the nineteenth century gave the British alternatives which the Americans did not have. The shifts among these alternatives, in this view, kept the early prison in England from monopolizing the penal sanctions as happened in the United States. Thus when the doctrinal disenchantment with the penitentiary intensified after the 1860s, it was inevitably more influential than any parallel American intellectual trend could have been.

There is considerable merit to this argument, but it cannot be the last word. It is true that the British after 1788 found a transportation alternative and that the Americans did not. However, it is also true that the Americans were made doctrinally unfriendly to transportation by their hostility to traditional British practices and by the search for a distinctively republican criminal justice that is described below. They chose imprisonment over other punishments because it fit their other values, not simply because they had no convenient alternatives. The clarity of hindsight must not be allowed to convert all analysis into retrospective determinism.

We have seen that construction of British prisons between 1780 and 1812 generally consisted of a small number of small county institutions, while the Americans built many famous large institutions and a body of theory to go with them. Despite the persistent overcrowding in its prisons, the United States experienced the 1820s and 1830s as great days for this social institution, whereas the British found little but disaster in the riots and typhus of Millbank. By the time of Tocqueville's tour of American prisons in the early 1830s, the Americans had had fifty years of developing belief, rhetoric, and (to them) successful experimentation. As late as the 1840s the British were, in a real sense, just getting started, and it was the later view of the Gladstone Committee that by 1857 the reformatory purpose—the institution's nominal best hope in the United States—had been "lost sight of." By 1863 the House of Lords Committee was making this official wisdom. In American terms, the doctrinal heyday of the British penitentiary was short indeed.

The British have always allowed and encouraged explicit, rationalist doctrines to determine their penal practices. As conventional wisdom changes, such doctrines are likely to be successively discarded, but social choices to do so are relatively easier to make. The American tradition has been more rooted in half-conscious, emotional commitments to the social institution of the prison. This is reflected in the greater influence of romantic and religious ideals on American attitudes to imprisonment. From the outset, the British seem to have been quite objective about the prison. In the popular imagination, they never fused the notions of imprisonment and punishment the way the Americans have always done. This fusion is the theme of the next chapter; it goes far to explain why the current British attack on rehabilitation may produce greater change than its counterpart in the United States. It shows also why the effort to fashion a new penal future for America is so wrenching for the makers of its public policy.

4 Theories and Symbols

Introduction

America is the land of technical pragmatism, and the inclination to see policy issues as technical problems pervades both its history and its contemporary culture. National pride in refusing to be ruled by abstract theory, combined with an insistence on incremental changes in response to current difficulties, has brought some great successes. But refusal to consider first principles can also bring great failures. Today's efforts to deal with prison problems are in danger of failing in just this way.

The tendency to flee from first principles dominates the correctional policymakers of the United States. They want desperately to believe that overcrowded, unsafe, and inhumane conditions can be treated as symptoms, without any attempt to understand the basic disorder. Legislators and administrators want to feel that the U.S. Court of Appeals for the Fifth Circuit was correct when, in considering a prisoner's rights case, it refused to enter what it called "the uncharted bog"[1] of the competing justifications for imprisonment. This is a fond hope, but it will not work, even for judges. Certainly, it' cannot work for other officials. The purposes of an institution are fundamental to any prescription for its reform. This is obvious, but it is usually ignored when those officials consider what to do about prisons. This chapter enters the bog that cannot be avoided in any serious discussion.

The best amphibious vehicle for this trip is an interpretative analysis of the historical patterns described above. The past weighs heavily on contemporary policymakers, who must act without offending traditions. Policy proposals often fail, not because they are examined and rejected but because society says implicitly, "We don't do things that way here." If our proposal in Chapter 5 is to have a chance, it must take account of these half-buried assumptions as well as of more explicit requirements. This chapter extends the argument that the American prison meets Eric Hobsbawm's standard for a powerful symbol: it represents something important in the imaginative life of the community.[2] To see this, we must consider more systematically than was possible in Chapter 3 the answers that different eras have given to the question, "Why should criminals be imprisoned?"

If historical interpretation is the best vehicle for reaching through to the contemporary debate, it is also a vehicle with some design defects. The controversy on the purposes of imprisonment has started to emit a white noise that is soporific to listeners and analysts alike. Too many tales of battles among those tired old horsemen— deterrence, incapacitation, retribution, and rehabilitation—have left us all eager for a new slant. These four venerable warriors cannot be abandoned completely, but their forces can be regrouped, and perhaps we can regard them in a new light. We can begin by considering the fundamental aims of the set of institutions, commonly lumped under the rubric of the criminal justice system, of which corrections is the final part.

Three Images of the Criminal Justice System

The criminal justice system administers the criminal law, whose aim, in Henry Hart's words, is to establish one of the "foundations for a tolerable and durable social order."[3] When a part of the system functions properly, it contributes to the social order; these contributions, however, are diverse, and to appreciate their full range a wide-angle lens is necessary. We must go beyond the obvious daily activities of the criminal justice system and consider its indirect contributions to social order as well as its direct ones. Only then can we see the full importance of the institution of imprisonment and the full difficulty of changing it.

We distinguish three constellations of these purposes. We emphasize that these are not mutually exclusive in practice; they are different ways of looking at the same activity. Each provides a useful perspective on the total process, from the passage of criminal laws to their application at the correctional tail of the system.

The first paradigm organizes criminal justice functions around the goal of "crime control." From this perspective, the central purpose of the criminal justice system is to reduce the number of offenses, and to do so by direct action. Three principal means are distinguished: (a) deterrence—making potential offenders refrain because they fear the consequences, (b) incapacitation—isolating the offender from society through imprisonment or banishment, (c) prevention—in which the opportunity to commit crimes is reduced by physical security measures.

The second paradigm may be called "legalist." From this perspective, the purpose of the criminal justice system is to articulate, embody, and reinforce the legal norms of the society. The legalists argue that even if a particular action by some part of the system makes no direct contribution to reducing the number of offenses, it may still perform a valuable social function. Criminal justice is regarded here as intended for the greater part of society that will obey the law, even as it anticipates a fraction that will break the law. The symbolism of the passage and administration of laws plays a vital part in this second image. Thus, for example, a legalist might perpetuate the myth that the U.S. Supreme Court is a completely nonpolitical body, because he feels that such social cement is more important than a realistic view of how the Court functions.

Punishment in general, imprisonment as its instrument, and policies such as restitution to victims are justified by many legalists as acts which satisfy the collective conscience. Legalists maintain that punishment for infractions of the criminal law is important not for its own sake, but as a distinguishable route to the goal of social order. Consider Salmond's classic statement of this view:

> Did we punish criminals merely from an intellectual appreciation of the expediency of so doing, and not because their crimes arouse in us the emotion of anger and the instinct of retribution, the criminal law would be but a feeble instrument. Indignation against injustice is, moreover, one of the chief constituents of the moral sense of the community, and positive morality is no less dependent on it than is the law itself. It is good, therefore, that such instincts and emotions should be encouraged and strengthened by their satisfaction; and in civilized societies this satisfaction is possible in any adequate degree only through the criminal justice of the state. There can be little question that at the present day the sentiment of retributive indignation is deficient rather than excessive, and requires stimulation rather than restraint.[4]

Of course, Durkheim and others have written of the function of law in the cohesion of society and the articulation of norms. The legalist rubric covers the sentiments which support this view, and it has been pasted with a variety of labels. Ernest van den Haag, for example, has spoken of the need to avoid the law-abiding citizen feeling cheated by impunity for the lawbreaker.[5] We use "legalist" here in a frankly reductive and utilitarian way, to describe such theorists who believe that for purposes of social cohesion punishment of criminals may often be justified even if it makes no direct contribution to the control of future crime.

Third is the "social service" paradigm. Here the criminal justice system and the correctional subsystem are seen as providing services to people whose criminal behavior stems from some unmet personal need. In different historical periods, these needs have included the opportunity for religious reflection, psychological counseling, job training, education, and so on. But the basic notion is that social order can be enhanced by the provision of social services through the criminal justice system. The modern instruments range from police shelters to court employment projects to the assistance provided by officers of probation and parole, whereas an eighteenth-century convict sermon saw the mere fact of imprisonment as conferring "a mutual benefit to the offender and that society against which the offense was committed."[6]

At some time in history, each of these images has played a part in guiding or reinforcing American criminal justice. Sometimes they influenced the actual practices of the institution, sometimes they provided crucial rhetorical justification for those practices. Their relative importance and solidity have changed from one era to another. At points in American history when their balance becomes unstable, the chance exists for fundamental change. We believe that the 1980s are a period of such flux. To support this claim, we must apply our three paradigms to the preceding chapter's outline of American penal history.

The Colonial Heritage

In American criminal justice before the Revolution, incarceration seems to be much less prominent than it is today. The jail was used to detain those awaiting trial, when it was feared they might otherwise run away. It also held offenders who had been convicted but not yet sentenced, and others who were detained while obligations such as debts were settled. But major offenders were rarely sent there as a sentence, and, with the exception described below, the practice of locking up serious criminals in order to reform them through social services was virtually unknown.

Capital punishment was provided for a wide range of offenses, including denying "the true God and His attributes," homosexual offenses, and the striking by a child of his natural father or mother. In the case of noncapital crimes a variety of forms of corporate punishment, including whipping, branding, mutilating, confinement in the stocks or pillory, and ducking were employed. Especially severe penalties were imposed for sexual crimes: "defiling the marriage bed," incest, bestiality, and bigamy could all be punished by life imprisonment. In *The Evolution of Penology in Pennsylvania*, Barnes notes that, under the original criminal code for His Majesty's American Colonies and Plantations, fornication "was punishable by fine, corporal punishment or marriage,"[7] presumably in order of severity.

In theory and in legislation, however, there was a forerunner of the social service paradigm in the colonial workhouse. The Massachusetts legislature, for example, passed in 1699 an "Act for Suppressing and Punishing Rogues, Vagabonds, Common Beggars . . . and for Setting the Poor to Work." In 1748 the New Jersey assembly authorized Middlesex County officials to build (in addition to a poorhouse) a workhouse that would also punish rogues, vagabonds, and petty criminals.[8] But as Rothman and others have noted, this theory of justification for incarceration did not have much effect. Many colonies that authorized workhouses for criminals provided no funds to build them, and those that were constructed tended to merge with the poorhouses in providing (irrespective of any criminal behavior) merely "a hospital for the poor."[9]

The house of correction seems virtually indistinguishable from the workhouse. Having located a source of social disorder in the "persons who wander about," who beg, insult, curse, and lie "to the corruption of manners . . . and the detriment of good order and religion,"[10] the Connecticut assembly called for the establishment of houses of correction that would restrain, set to work, and punish these persons. Although vagabonds and idlers were taken seriously, they were clearly less dangerous to an orderly community than robbers, burglars, and murderers. Under whatever name, the incarcerative institutions of the colonies were not expected to deal with major criminals.

Why? In the terms of our three models of criminal justice, a superficial answer is that legalist needs were met by the stigmatizing punishments of the stocks, the pillory, branding, and ducking; and crime control needs were met by fines, whipping, banishment, and capital punishment. But there are less obvious explanations. Rothman's attempt is only partly persuasive when he maintains that "given their conception of deviant behavior and institutional organizations, they did not believe that a jail could rehabilitate or intimidate or detain the offender."[11] Despite the frequency of escapes from colonial jails, it is hard to believe that the colonists doubted their own ability to construct a building that would contain offenders if containment was seriously intended. More plausible is that crime control through confinement seemed simply unnecessary; with expulsion as an option, why need the colonists bear the costs of incarcerative institutions whose effects were the same?

On surer ground is Rothman's view that the colonists were pessimistic about achieving social order through the servicing of the unmet needs of criminals. He notes, "They placed little faith in the possibility of reform. Prevailing Calvinist doctrines that stressed the natural depravity of man and the powers of the devil hardly allowed

such optimism. Since temptations to misconduct were not only om-
nipresent but practically irresistible, rehabilitation could not serve as
the basis for a prison program."[12] If the ultimate source of deviance
lay not in social institutions but in the individual offender himself,
and if, furthermore, that source was divinely created, there was little
hope for creating a new environment (such as a prison) which could
transform the deviant into a law-abiding citizen. Minor aberrations
could be punished—because they were wrong, not because they
could be corrected—in the community by fines, corporal punishment,
or humiliation. Major and repeated offenses had to be matched by the
extreme measure of expulsion from the community, or by death.

It is unfashionable today to speak kindly of colonial criminal justice. Capital, corporal, and shaming punishments are regarded as
regressive, fiscal penalties as ineffective, banishment as irrelevant to
contemporary legal and political realities. Moreover, some say that
the colonial system had a serious lack of punishments actually
applied in the middle range. Vacillation between extremes of le-
niency and severity are said to have made justice unpredictable, so
that an offender might escape punishment after several convictions
and then "abruptly he ended up on the gallows."[13]

A case can be made, however, that compared with today's
America, the colonists had a well-calibrated and subtle system of
criminal justice. They separated the question of social service from
that of criminal penalties and generally did not use the workhouse or
the house of correction to make over the serious offender. They
helped the poor because the poor needed help; entry to the poorhouse
was not forced. To be sure, the line between legalist and crime control motives is always hard to draw. To the colonial legalist, law
enforcement was justified in part on the grounds that the laws were
ultimately God's laws and to fail to enforce them would compound the
ill by offending against Him. The public and humiliating punishments do suggest a desire to achieve a crime control purpose as well,
through the deterrence of other potential offenders. But, given the
deep religious character of the American colonies, there is no reason
to doubt the legalists' sincerity in maintaining that laws had to be
enforced partly because divinely ordained norms had been violated
and that these norms dictated a certain amount of expiatory punishment. This idea was inseparable from the justification of law enforcement as an instrument of secular social order.

The mixture of purposes within the colonies is seen in the practice
of both whipping and expelling certain offenders. Usually applied to
nonresident robbers and burglars, the dual punishment may be regarded as serving both legalist and crime control needs: corporal
punishment for the former, banishment for the latter. We can dismiss

the suggestion that the colonists did not think of supplementing or replacing such practices with incarceration. Most legislators simply regarded its special contribution—incapacitation followed by the criminal's return to the community—as irrelevant to their conceptions of a just and stable order. That they consciously rejected it is shown by the uniqueness of the seventeenth-century experiment of William Penn. Revolted by sanguinary punishments and convinced that capital punishment in particular was grossly overused—fully 20 percent of colonial punishments were capital—Penn turned to imprisonment as America's first diversion project. Other colonies refused to follow, and the innovation was not pressed even in Pennsylvania when opposed by the British Parliament in 1717.[14] Graeme Newman has said that imprisonment is the price America paid whenever it tried to abolish capital punishment.[15] This has been true in a variety of ways, economic and symbolic. With Penn's exception, colonial America did not find acceptable the price of this expensive, nonpublic, incapacitative punishment.

The Postrevolutionary Prison

The Revolutionary War and formative period of the Constitution mark the first shift in the balance of purposes of American criminal justice. In the aftermath of independence, Americans rejected the old punitive laws and rapidly amended their criminal codes; we saw above that the pattern was exemplified in Pennsylvania, where the code revision of 1786 led first to the adoption of public punishment at hard labor and later to the reform of the Walnut Street Jail. "Armed with patriotic fervor, sharing a repugnance for things British,"[16] the Americans were driven to find not only new laws but new institutions to implement the laws.

This impulse was strongest concerning capital punishment, which Americans associated with the form of government they had just thrown off. Even some Englishmen felt that before the Revolution public hangings were rare in the American colonies "because the people had a hand in the making of the laws."[17] Benjamin Rush, the American Quaker, charged that capital penalties were "the natural offspring of monarchical government," whereas republican governments "speak a very different language. They appreciate human life and increase public and private obligations to preserve it."[18] Except for a few very serious crimes (in some states, except only for first degree murder), the abolition of the death penalty was a principal feature of most of the new postrevolutionary codes.

Objecting in principle both to the public corporal punishments of earlier eras and to transportation, the Americans chose to expand the role of incarceration. At first, the full significance of this shift may not have been appreciated. In the late 1770s and 1780s, it was not widely recognized that the elimination of capital punishment might eventually require the provision of a great system of penal institutions and the systematic regulation of their administration. Those who initiated what Paul Tappan called "the movement toward mass imprisonment of offenders that soon became worldwide"[19] did not realize that that was what they were doing. But this fusion of the general desire for a distinctively American way of punishing and the specific institution of imprisonment is essential for an understanding of the prison's deep hold on the nation's imagination. Moreover, this development merged in turn with the religious optimism of the new nation. As Ignatieff was quoted above, the early American prison was powerfully influenced by the Quaker hope for a reformation of convicts that would parallel "the spiritual awakening of a believer." Postrevolutionary America was not nearly so modest about the new institution as some modern commentators would have us believe.

We dissent here from an element of Rothman's excellent work on the "Discovery of the Asylum." Rothman maintains that late eighteenth-century America had great hopes for deterrence once the criminal law was legislated with subtlety and applied with certainty, but that little was expected from the design and programs of the prison itself. In this view, few people considered how to organize a prison, because legislators felt that "to pass the proper laws would end the problem."[20] The prison is presented as an almost incidental adjunct to a criminal justice system dominated by what we have called the crime control paradigm.

Our dissent is a matter of emphasis in the balance of purposes and hopes for the early American prison. It is true that the emergence of incarceration as a criminal penalty stemmed initially from some broader hopes for the new criminal law. A Calvinist pessimism about social engineering was yielding to the Enlightenment view of the potential deviant as a rational being who would calculate the costs of breaking the law. Thus, a system of penalties had to be finely calibrated in theory and applied with certainty in practice. This general idea had to meet other specific conditions. Calculation of the appropriate punishment must be possible in advance of the offender's action. Also, penalties must not have the unintended effect of escalating misbehavior. Under earlier systems, as Beccaria had seen, "the severity of punishment of itself emboldens men to commit the very wrong it is supposed to prevent. They are driven to commit additional crimes to avoid the punishment for a single one."[21] And finally, the postrevolutionary revulsion against corporal and capital punishments prohibited the reintroduction of the sanguinary penalties.

What innovation could meet all these conditions? Banishment was not a possibility on a large scale. A growing consciousness of belonging to a state that was in turn part of a nation made it archaic simply to banish an offender from a town. Since criminal justice was a state and local matter, the option of international deportation did not arise. To a society in search of a new criminal justice based on the crime control paradigm, imprisonment had everything to recommend it. It could use long sentences to deal with the serious criminals who had traditionally received capital punishment or expulsion, and short sentences to deal with the minor offenders who frequently escaped any punishment at all. However, crime control purposes alone could never have sustained imprisonment as the punishment of choice that it soon became. As we showed in the previous chapter, their prison did not emerge solely from Americans' adoption of Enlightenment theory. Their use of the prison as an instrument of social order went beyond pure crime control, and their other motives must be sought in our two other paradigms of criminal justice.

In the justification for the postrevolutionary prison, the social service purpose played a larger part than is sometimes acknowledged. The reformers at Walnut Street did consider in detail how to organize a prison. In these days of high Quaker influence the emphasis on using social institutions to make better men is to be expected. The organization of the penitentiary was a means to this end. As described earlier, there was a clear doctrinal basis for the Pennsylvania innovation of single-occupancy cells. Isolated in these cells, serious criminals were kept from further corrupting each other, and this part of the prison (the penitentiary house) was separated from the rest of the inmate population. Moral and religious instruction and formal chapel services were part of the routine. The reform of criminals was a central aim, and it was claimed that the aim had been achieved: Because of the successful organization of the penitentiary, said Caleb Lownes in Philadelphia in 1793, "We lie down in peace, we sleep in security."[22]

New York's pattern was much the same, its hopes as high, its claims as great. Consider the modest expectations of Thomas Eddy, the designer and warden of New York's 1796 Newgate prison. His creation, said Eddy, would "become a durable monument of the wisdom, justice, and humanity of its own legislators, more glorious than the most splendid achievements of conquerors or kings; and be remembered when the magnificent structures of folly and pride, with their founders, are alike exterminated and forgotten."[23]

Eddy distinguished among hardened offenders, criminals who retained some sense of virtue, and young persons convicted for the first time. This mandated individualized treatment, since in his view "the reformation of the offender was the chief end of punishment." Although crime control purposes such as deterrence might play a part, he saw this as "momentary and uncertain." His primary goal was "eradicating the evil passions and corrupt habits which are the sources of guilt."[24] Religious instruction and a night school for which the student-felons paid four shillings worth of extra labor were among the social services provided by this early correctional facility. Disruptive prisoners were kept in solitary cells, and the school was open only to the well-behaved. The design and program of the prison *were* of concern to postrevolutionary Americans. Among justifying purposes of incarceration, social service provided crucial support for crime control during the prison's formative years.

The legalist dimension completes the picture. As the strands described above merged during the years between the Revolution and the early nineteenth century, the prison came to stand virtually alone as the symbol of humane, just punishment. Its religious ideology, its encouragement of visitors, fortified its place in what Ignatieff has called a shared moral universe. The crucial links between imprisonment and punishment were forged much earlier than sometimes acknowledged. Orlando Lewis saw this almost sixty years ago; the first American prisons, he wrote, "started with the proposition of segregating their supposedly most difficult and dangerous cases. The single cells were thus at the outset *branded in the public mind* as punishment cells, for the protection of society and for the infliction of the hardest endurable conditions."[25] This equation contrasts with the British formative period, when capital punishment and transportation were used for serious crime and imprisonment for minor property offenders.

It is idle to assign relative weights in this process to the desire for a distinctively American system of justice, the revulsion against capital and other sanguinary penalties, and the telescoping of the symbols of Enlightenment rationalism and humane justice. But if we are correct that the prison had become the symbol of legitimate criminal punishment in America long before Jackson, there are implications for the current policy debate. In our view, the early branding in the public mind—that serious punishment means imprisonment—remains a powerful legacy. People almost reflexively resist change in a social institution which has been "ever thus." But in the 1970s, other critics of imprisonment began to use a different view of history as an agent of change. They tried to liberate modern America from the idea that prisons always have been and always will be with us. Once Americans see that the United States created this institution, ran the argument, they will see that there is nothing absolute about it. Moreover, the more recent its invention, the easier it should be to shift to some other system of punishment; thus there was a strong incentive to date the origins of the contemporary penitentiary as late as possible and to deny that the prison is as deeply entrenched in American society as we believe it to be.

There is room for honest disagreement here, but to underestimate the difficulty of change is sometimes to lower the chance of achieving it. If our view of history is correct, then this difficulty was and remains very great, and past failures to achieve change are easily comprehensible. Except for their ambivalent and intermittent support of capital punishment, Americans have *always* given imprisonment a monopoly over other forms of serious punishment. It has always been the currency of American criminal justice. To acknowledge this is not a counsel of pessimism but of realism. All the traditions and values heaped onto the institution of imprisonment must be considered in any efforts to alter it. In the formative years of the institution, between 1776 and the early 1800s, these included the aims of social service and legalism as well as conventional crime control. This solid, balanced foundation goes far in explaining why later generations have found the superstructure so hard to change.

The "Monomanie" of the Penitentiary

Our view of the postrevolutionary prison influences our treatment of subsequent developments. Because we see the main lines of the social institution as already established by the very early nineteenth century, we take a less expansive view than other observers of many later events. Some, for example, see the 1820s as a major turning point in American criminal justice. Others maintain that during Andrew Jackson's presidency the Pennsylvania-Auburn controversy remained a fundamental threat to a fledgling institution of imprisonment; in this view, only when this battle subsided did pessimism about the prison's efficacy give way to real optimism.

We agree that by the early 1820s there was deep concern over crowding, indiscriminate use of the pardon to control populations, and the failure to reform inmates. Although in 1813 Eddy's colleagues claimed to have evidence that was "decisive proof of the efficacy of the system, and highly consolatory to the patriot and the philanthropist,"[26] three years later Newgate contained more than double the number it was designed to hold, and in 1818 the last in a series of annual riots was so severe that the military had to fire into the yard to put it down. (The parallel with Attica will not be lost on contemporary readers.) However, the inference drawn was not that the institution of imprisonment should be abandoned in favor of some other criminal penalty but rather that the design and program of the physical facility were at fault. The largest investigation of the period saw the central problem in the failure to follow earlier principles of classification and organization: "Convicts of all ages, and all degrees of turpitude, have been placed together, and all the evil and fatal consequences of vicious communications have been exhibited.... Your Committee need appeal to no documents, to show the total want of a proper division of convicts in our Penitentiary." As a result, "morals, instead of being improved, are broken down."[27]

There followed, of course, the famous debate between the Pennsylvania theorists, who argued that the proper division of inmates could be achieved only by solitary cells, and the Auburn theorists, who hoped to break "vicious communications" by combining solitary sleeping quarters with congregate labor performed in silence. Both positions were refinements of design rather than fundamental attacks on the institution of imprisonment. True, there were individual administrators so dismayed by conditions that they recommended the supplement of a federal penal colony in the Pacific Northwest, or other forms of transportation to a particular area of New York State, but none of these alternatives was ever seriously considered by any state legislature. The dominance of the prison as both instrument and symbol of just punishment was merely increased by the enormous public interest and hope placed in the controversy between Pennsylvania and Auburn.

This controversy was in fact a rather one-sided affair. While the two sides may have battled evenly in the number of pamphlets issued, the balance was largely rhetorical. In the entire United States, only three Pennsylvania penitentiaries were ever built. This was partly for reasons of cost; the Eastern State Penitentiary in Pennsylvania was at its completion in 1829 the most expensive building ever constructed in the country. Also, most legislators found it redundant to erect concrete walls around individual prisoners when they could be kept from communicating with each other in less elaborate ways. Legislators soon learned that those few prisons that did start out as "pure Pennsylvania" were, within a short time, forced to hold two and three men in cells that had been intended for one.

In the Auburn system, which came to dominate American practice, a new balance was struck among crime control, social service, and legalism. The Pennsylvania system had high hopes for the social service paradigm; these were based on the idea of useful solitary labor in an uncorrupted environment. There the offender could reflect upon his sins and emerge without the inclination to commit new crimes. Auburn, quite explicitly, adopted a different view: "The great end and design of criminal law, is the prevention of crimes, *through fear of punishment; the reformation of offenders being a minor consideration*" (emphasis added). The prison should be not "a mere place of good living and light punishment, but a place of dread and terror." The Auburn inspectors felt that "the fear of punishment operates on a whole community; the means of reformation on a few individuals."[28]

With the emergence of Auburn as the dominant model, there came an explicit dominance of crime control and retributivist motives over the hopes for indirect influence through social service. While in Auburn's formative period reformers such as Gershom Powers and Louis Dwight maintained that religious and educational rebuilding could follow the breaking of the prisoner's will, the harsher view of Elam Lynds informed most of the emerging state systems. Warden at Auburn (in the days when wardens were very public figures) and builder of Sing Sing with Auburn convict labor, Lynds was an administrator of whom one historian has said, "It is difficult to avoid concluding that cruelty was part of his makeup."[29] Nonetheless, he was greatly admired, even by such Quaker reformers as Eddy, who felt Lynds had "those peculiar qualifications, that will enable him to carry the penitentiary to a degree of perfection that it has never yet attained."[30] Lynds's model of American imprisonment was the crime control model—deterrence of future offenses outside the prison by making life inside it one of dread and terror—with a little symbolic humiliation thrown in for good measure.

Bizarre inmate uniforms were an example of an Auburn legalism which continued a long tradition of symbolic ceremonies of degradation. Although the striped outfits have sometimes been justified as a deterrent to escapes, surely it has legalist significance that "although the convicts were forbidden visitors of their own, citizens who paid a fee could come to the prison and look at them much as if they were animals in a zoo."[31] Such practices seem not only consistent with, but also intended to fulfill, legalist purposes. If criminal punishment is intended in part for the law-abiding as well as the law-breaking, and there must be some process for reinforcing norms with consequences that can be seen, imprisonment has a major weakness; it is out of the public eye. One American reaction has been to ritualize other, earlier stages in the criminal process, such as the trial. The practice of prisoner "viewings" can be regarded as another embodiment of the same legalist impulse.

In general, however, such supplements were not necessary to maintain the legalist pillar of the nineteenth-century American prison. The fusion of criminal justice purposes that had crystallized in the postrevolutionary penitentiary was not seriously threatened. With rare exceptions in rhetoric and fewer in practice, locking offenders up remained the punishment of choice. The men who founded Auburn in 1816 had "a determination to conserve established institutions, including the penitentiary, and not an impulse to originate something new and different."[32] Some historians argue that with the development of the congregate system in the mid-1820s the Auburn administrators found it "necessary to innovate in order to conserve."[33] However, they innovated within the framework of an established social institution. Strengthened by even greater nationalist sentiments after the War of 1812, reinforced by new and distinctively American theories of reform, the prison was rock-solid by the mid-nineteenth century. Like any enduring institution, it commanded support from different quarters for different reasons. Criminal justice officials felt it served crime control purposes, while the public added the motivations of legalism and at least the rhetoric of social service.

That many administrators failed to share the public's social service hopes is worth emphasis, because some modern observers see the Jacksonians as mindlessly utopian. Rothman speaks of their "incredible optimism," of their hope "to eradicate crime from the new world," and says that "no one questioned" the penitentiary's fundamental premise that it could make good citizens out of bad ones.[34] There was, however, an undercurrent of skepticism. Moreover, the skeptics and pessimists consisted largely of those entitled by experience or close study to an informed opinion. The commissioner of the Maryland penitentiary, for example, felt that "from a closer and more intimate view of the subject, I have rather abandoned a hope I once entertained, of the general reformation of offenders through the penitentiary system. I now think its chief good is in the prevention of crime by the confinement of criminals."[35] The district attorney of New York said in 1831, "As for the penitentiaries, I believe their discipline excellent in that it maintains admirable order in the prison and renders the labour of the inmates productive; but I do not believe in its power to alter a man's tendencies and habits. In general, I do not believe that the adult criminal reforms, however one goes about it. My opinion is that he comes out of our penitentiaries hardened."[36]

We could lengthen the list of skeptics. Indeed, when Tocqueville came to America to assess the prisons, he made just such a list. His diary divided expert opinion into "those who believe in the moral reform of adult prisoners," "those who do not believe in it," and "those who doubt it." At the time of the diary entry there were still no names in the first column. Tocqueville stressed that the "belief in the ineffectiveness of the penitentiary system for moral reform has appeared up to now to be shared by a great number of other very capable men, among others by the practical men." Summing up, he gave at best a draw to those who felt social services could justify imprisonment: "We have the materials to prove that the penitentiary system reforms and that it does not reform."[37]

Like all visitors at the time, Beaumont and Tocqueville were struck by America's optimism about "seizing the future."[38] This optimism, they said, had focused in a class of professional reformers who "have caught the monomanie of the penitentiary system, which to them seems the remedy for all the evils of society." Tocqueville's view of these reformers combined incredulity and sarcasm: "Starting from abstractions which deviate more or less from reality, they consider man, however far advanced in crime, as still susceptible of being brought back to virtue.... They hope for an epoch when all criminals may be radically reformed, the prisons be entirely empty, and justice find no crimes to punish."[39]

It is clear from the tone that Beaumont and Tocqueville had not caught the monomanie. Ultimately they sided with the crime control justifications of the "practical men." Feeling that the theories on the reform of the prisoners were "vague and uncertain," they allowed that "there is another kind of reformation" that the penitentiary could produce. This might be less thorough than that which produced a truly good man, but yet useful for society. The first object of punishment, they felt, is "to teach him to obey," and this the discipline of the prison seemed competent to do: "Perhaps, leaving the prison he is not an honest man, but... without loving virtue, he may detest the crime of which he has suffered the cruel consequences, and if he is not more virtuous he has become at least more judicious; his morality is not honor, but interest.... If he has not become in truth better, he is at least more obedient to the laws, and that is all which society has the right to demand."[40]

Beaumont and Tocqueville also gave some support to the social service paradigm. They thought the penitentiary could teach an idler an honest occupation and an ignorant man to read and write. But by the standards of the day, this was hardly a ringing defense; the system wanted to stand or fall on its ability to reform men, and this Beaumont and Tocqueville doubted. "If the penitentiary system cannot propose to itself an end other than radical reformation... the legislature perhaps should abandon this system; not because the aim is not an admirable one, but because it is too rarely obtained."[41] Thus the most extensive study of the American penitentiary, at its peak of optimism, rejected the central purposive justification. It was cold comfort to the system's advocates that the French critics shored up the structure with an argument based not on reform but on deterrence. In the 1980s some maintain that reform and deterrence are indistinguishable in effect. But the Americans of the nineteenth century did not see it that way, and those who saw Tocqueville's report were more than a little dismayed.

Backing and Filling in the Purposes Debate

The skepticism of Tocqueville's practical men did not keep the social service image from exerting a powerful pull on theoreticians and reformers. From one historical era to another, hopes for reform were shunted in practice from one new supplementary institution to another. Tocqueville himself acted in this tradition. Having expected to find Sing Sing "the most perfect penitentiary in the United States,"[42] he found that "moral influence is disregarded" and that "the directors of the establishment seemed to have in view the support of external order only, and the passive obedience of the convicts."[43] So Tocqueville shifted much of his enthusiasm to the house of refuge for children and adolescents. In his view, even potentially wayward youths could be incarcerated before they had been arrested or convicted of anything. And since no one could predict how long regeneration would take, such confinements should be of indefinite rather than definite length.

The Reformatory movement of the 1860s and 1870s illustrates the same pattern. Recognition of the failures of the adult penitentiary either to cure crime, to reform the inmate, or even to devise a rational system of classification led to an effort to prune away part of the inmate population. In this scheme, offenders who were older than the juveniles in the houses of refuge, but were arguably not yet hardened criminals, were to be segregated in special facilities, given indeterminate sentences, and reformed. Elmira, in New York State, emerged in 1877 as the model for a proposed system. Its planners emphasized that the legislation "does not contemplate simply another State Prison.... In referring to a reformatory we assume that... there should be a selection from the mass of convicted criminals, of such persons as are most likely to yield to reformatory influence.... No person (should) be sentenced to the proposed reformatory whose age is less than sixteen or more than thirty years, or who shall be known to have been previously convicted of any felonious offense."[44] The commissioners also recommended a test for the theory that "criminals should be sentenced not for a definite term of years, as at present, but until they are reformed, which may, of course, turn out to be for life."[45]

The Reformatory's pruning did nothing to arrest the post–Civil War trend of rising prison populations and deteriorating conditions. As shown in Chapter 3, crowding was worse in the postwar years than at any previous time in the penitentiary period; even token efforts at rehabilitation were abandoned. By the end of the nineteenth century the rhetorical flourishes of administrators had become a sham and the system something of a scandal. But the tenacity of the social service image can be seen in the late nineteenth and early twentieth-century

Progressive innovations of probation and parole. The Progressives explicitly rejected the traditional Auburn legalism. "Revenge and its modern outgrowth, punishment, belong to the past of legal history,"[46] Pound wrote. The way to success, he said, lay in "the fullest team play" between legal and other social agencies. Preventive criminal justice would identify disruptive individuals at an early stage, and at least allow prisons to become residual institutions rather than social control mechanisms of choice. We saw earlier that compared with his British contemporaries, Pound remained relatively optimistic about the ability of the prison and its adjuncts to provide social service.

Again, however, the divergence was immense between the declared purposes of the system and its practice. As the Reformatory principles of the 1870s were never widely or systematically applied, so probation did not resemble its theoretical descriptions of intense supervision and service. It may have served some legalist needs by applying a largely symbolic, nonincarcerative sentence. Parole, although defended on the ground that it could calibrate the time in prison needed for rehabilitation, in fact induced the type of manipulative hypocrisy predicted by Tocqueville, and generally also failed to provide real service. What explains the persistence of the social service rhetoric when administrators made no serious attempt to apply it? Why did American Progressives fail to achieve the curtailment of incarceration rates that occurred in England during these years? In his survey of the Progressive era, Rothman finds that answer in the inertia and hypocrisy of the judicial and administrative bureaucracies.[47] There is truth in this, but more can be said. An examination of the Progressives' failure provides a summary background of the history of debates about the prison's purpose from the Revolution almost to the present.

By the end of the eighteenth century, American criminal justice possessed three things that had been absent in colonial days: optimism about achieving social order through crime control (specifically, through deterrence), a fusion of those hopes with legalist and social service aspirations, and a physical plant that was both an instrument and a symbol of that optimism. In the buildings at Walnut Street, New Jersey, and Newgate, built in the 1790s, the prison brought together the three images of criminal justice. The merging of these three sets of values was not inevitably determined by the nation's economic or social structure; it resulted from a particular mixture of contingent ideas and circumstances. But after emerging from that formative period, the American prison was already loaded with legalist significance long before Jackson's presidency. Then, and in all later eras except for the present, revisionism became "tinkering only" because dismantling the institution of imprisonment was not seriously considered. Reform groups have always been on the fringe, because they attacked only the wings of crime control ("Prisons don't deter") or social service ("Prisons don't reform"). The legalist consensus, on which the institution ultimately rests, has until recently been too broad and too strong to allow major change.

The Progressives, then, discovered and demonstrated the power of the prison in American life. They tinkered with the rhetoric, changing the nominal balance of purposes, but had little effect on practice. They found the prison's symbolic strength to be so great that it not only perpetuated itself but also made other punishments seem ludicrous. To the present day, many American listeners smile tolerantly when they hear about Progressive reforms. Similarly, they are reflexively hostile to suggestions that nonincarcerative penalties from other times or cultures be examined. To America, real punishment *means* prison.

In this light, the Progressives' difficulties can be better understood. True, they combined high-minded social service rhetoric with half-hearted practical efforts; but they were trying to change an institution that reflected a deep, often unstated consensus. To see their divergence of purposes and practices as the behavior of hypocritical and self-serving bureaucrats is correct but too narrow. Throughout American history, imprisonment has relied principally on its legalist pillar; the battle between its crime control and social service purposes has gone on for 200 years over the heads of the legalists. What is new in the debate of the 1980s is that the legalist consensus itself has been broken. Many thoughtful and influential legalists have concluded that the need for a humane, order-producing system of punishment is not being met by the prison. For them the prison has come to symbolize precisely the opposite: irrational, unprincipled, arbitrary, inhumane punishment. The central support of any social institution, its moral legitimacy, has been severely weakened. But for almost two centuries this pillar was so strong that shifts in the balance between the other two supports, crime control and social service, did not change the practice of the institution or threaten its future.

The Contemporary Purposes Debate

The weight of the legalist tradition has been a primary constraint on America's ability to choose criminal justice innovations. Beaumont and Tocqueville felt the choice was limited to "a bad system of imprisonment"[48] or the penitentiary, and they translated this into a choice between Auburn and Pennsylvania. Today's debate is straining to broaden the options, to create a choice in a particular case among imprisonment and a wide range of other penalties. Only the recent split in the legalist party gives us hope for breaking the mythic link between punishment and imprisonment that America has forged over the last two hundred years.

The crucial change has been that attacks on the social service wing of imprisonment have penetrated to its legalist core. In the contemporary debate, there are two quite different assaults on social service as a justification for incarceration: on its efficacy and on its legitimacy. We have shown that the first is not new. Although more widespread today, doubts that the purpose of reform could be achieved are as old as the penitentiary itself. But the attack on the legitimacy of purposive incarceration—on the idea that a society should or may lock up an offender in order to reform him—*is* new.

This assault on legitimacy maintains that even if the goal of rehabilitating inmates could be achieved, it should not be attempted; it is a morally wrong exercise of governmental power to incarcerate someone for the purpose of reforming him. "'Rehabilitation,' whatever it means and whatever the programs that allegedly give it meaning, must cease to be a purpose of the prison sanction," writes Norval Morris.[49] Elsewhere he uses the argument from ineffectiveness as well, but here Morris argues from moral principle rather than from any assessment of "what works":

> The rejection of that model of treatment... as a part of crime control flows not from lack of power or competence to influence the criminal's behavior but from historical evidence about the misuse of power and from more fundamental views of the nature of man and his rights to freedom. These properly limit the power that we wish to accord the state over the individual.... we do not reject "the individualized treatment model," because human behavior cannot be changed by the actor in collaboration with others assisting him in that change.... The fallacy lies in the reliance on its coercive application *outside the proper constraints of a due respect for human rights*. [Emphasis added][50]

In a similar vein, David Rothman argues that social service must be abandoned as a purpose of incarceration because "the concept of rehabilitation simply legitimates too much." While acknowledging that the "noble lie" of rehabilitation has been tactically useful in such areas as prisoners' rights litigation, Rothman feels that the ethical dangers of other applications, ranging from an extension of time served in prison to chemotherapy and psychosurgery, are intolerable.[51] Whereas Morris believes in truly voluntary and facilitative programs, Rothman doubts these could occur in correctional settings without abuses that create more ethical problems than they solve.

Both share a belief in a fundamental right not to be rehabilitated; Rothman is pessimistic about the ability or inclination of correctional administrators to protect that right. Both would agree with David Greenberg's striking summary: "The desire to help, when coupled with the desire to control, is totalitarian."[52]

This [...]ny contemporary [...]ment and a symbol [...]itomizes all that is [...]nprincipled coercio[...] saw above that in [...]ed the symbol of S[...]s is crucial. Prisons[...]itimate but ineffect[...]he political fringe; [...]he political center.

The l[...]nal wing of their pa[...]heavily on a readin[...]iminal laws more ef[...]sing prison populati[...]it, Herman Kahn s[...]ptable currency o[...]k between punishment and prison is by no means abandoned. Yet some revisionist legalists do not understand the continuing strength of traditionalist legalism. For example, the American Friends Service Committee says, "We believe there is much to be gained from honesty in our semantics. By characterizing all penal coercion as punishment, we emphasize rather than dilute the critical necessity of limiting it as much as possible . . . . Punishment is at best a necessary evil; we regard the punishing power as society's "last resort," to be used only where imperatively required and when no other less stringent measures of education and social control will suffice."[56] These contemporary Quakers feel that once punishment is acknowledged as the sole justification for imprisonment, fewer people will be locked up. However, the American Friends Service Committee fails to recognize the power of the legalist notion that punishment is not a necessary evil but a positive good. Salmond's statement about the instinct of retribution, quoted above,[57] provides an eloquent example of this view. Such sentiments as his, tied to traditional American attitudes to imprisonment, remain strong in the contemporary debate. The legalists today are divided; while some see the prison as symbolic of illegitimate coercive power, others strongly disagree. The weakening of the prison's moral foundation makes change possible, but the out-

[Handwritten margin note:] But help who? Help prisoners, or others through prisoners? Is the argument here against corporal punishment & for bodily integrity?

come is by no means clear. Indeed, we shall argue later that the result of all this turmoil could just as easily be a penal system that is worse rather than better than today's.

Crime Control as a Justifying Aim

With the weakening of both social service and legalism as justifying purposes of imprisonment, crime control today bears an increased burden. Traditionally, it leaned most heavily on the concept of deterrence. Defenders of the prison had always assumed it a common-sense proposition that something as unpleasant as incarceration would inhibit potential offenders. In the 1960s this assumption was challenged, and by 1973 the National Advisory Commission on Criminal Justice Standards and Goals was declaring flatly that prisons "do not deter."[58] In its turn, this dictum was examined with more sophisticated statistical methods, and in 1981 it must be regarded as an open question.

A special panel of the National Academy of Sciences, concluding the most extensive survey of the matter, has said that "we cannot yet assert that the evidence warrants an affirmative conclusion regarding deterrence," but warned that this "[does] not imply . . . that deterrence does not exist, since the evidence certainly favors a proposition supporting deterrence more than it favors one asserting that deterrence is absent."[59] It is likely that the question will remain open, or more accurately, open and shut and open again. This has been the pattern with studies of capital punishment, with the conventional wisdom shifting from "Capital punishment laws do not deter"[60] to "But executions do"[61] to "We really don't know."[62] Moreover, each time one of these shifts takes place, a whole set of expectations and preconceived opinions crystallize around it. By themselves the statistical data on deterrence are never likely to be strong enough to support the crime control pillar of imprisonment. One reason is that the deterrent effects of imprisonment are inevitably confounded with the incapacitative effects. A negative association between crime and imprisonment represents the two effects combined, and currently most statisticians have no confidence in their ability to separate the two.

Among justifications for imprisonment the best hope for the crime control model in recent years has been pure incapacitation. Even the National Advisory Commission acknowledged that there had to be some reduction in crime against the general society by men and women who are locked up.[63] Indeed, with the current weakness of all the other defenses of the prison, it is not surprising that incapacitation has become the stalwart. However, there are some major difficulties here as well. Even among honest statisticians, there is deep controversy over the extent of the incapacitative effects.[64] And even if we could resolve finally the methodological and quantitative problems of these studies, important concerns would remain.

Broad-brush justifications of imprisonment, such as "only to incapacitate" or "only to do justice" are hard to apply consistently. The National Council on Crime and Delinquency, for example, has argued that "confinement is necessary only for the offender who, if not confined, would be a serious danger to the public. For all others, who are not dangerous and who constitute the great majority of offenders, the sentence of choice should be one or another of the wide variety of noninstitutional dispositions."[65] Who is dangerous? In its Model Sentencing Act of 1972, the NCCD defined two types of dangerous offenders: the offender who has committed a serious crime against a person and shows a behavior pattern of persistent assaultiveness based on serious mental disturbance, and the offender deeply involved in organized crime.[66] It broadened the definition in 1977.[67] But whatever the specific content given to the concept, dangerousness as a basis for incarceration involves a liberal group such as NCCD in logical difficulties. To a great extent, these are the same critics who attack purposive rehabilitation, the indeterminate sentence, and the institution of parole on the grounds that no one can predict future offender behavior. Yet the use of dangerousness as a basis for incarceration implies a prediction about his future behavior.

It is not possible to have it both ways. If one cannot predict behavior, how can incapacitation and dangerousness be used as a basis for public policy of any kind? Many liberals are searching for a principle that will reduce incarceration to a residual role in American justice, but if they want to use incapacitation for this purpose they must abandon their absolute opposition to the notion of dangerousness. As more liberals realize this, many have been driven to bury their predictions of dangerousness in a theory that justifies imprisonment on other grounds. The doctrine of just deserts is becoming a favored hiding place.

Deserting Desert

The liberal search for a principle to limit the use of imprisonment has increasingly centered on the concept of desert. Norval Morris, for example, has argued that "no sanction should be imposed greater than that which is deserved by the last crime, or series of crimes, for which the offender is being sentenced."[68] Believing that "prediction of future criminality is an unjust basis for determining that the convicted criminal should be imprisoned,"[69] Morris finds in desert a principle that can indicate not which punishment *must* be imposed but which punishment *may* be imposed. Other liberals, however, use desert to determine when imprisonment is mandated. Andrew von Hirsch, for example, attempts this in *Doing Justice*[70]; Morris calls this the use of desert as a defining rather than limiting principle.

Although in the next chapter we shall disagree with Morris about the matter of dangerousness, our hisorical analysis makes us prefer his use of desert to that of von Hirsch. Every analyst is of course free to use a concept in his own way, but there are risks. In our view, von Hirsch perpetuates the traditional fusion of punishment and imprisonment. The principle of desert does not imply incarceration, or any other particular punishment. Liberals who perpetuate that fusion will be constantly vulnerable to having their principle co-opted by others who agree that punishment implies imprisonment but feel that most crimes deserve more of both rather than less. The risk is compounded in von Hirsch's Modified Desert Model, which allows incapacitation to justify deviations from deserved severity.[71]

Liberal legalists are searching for a conceptual tool to undermine traditional practices on imprisonment, but they may be asking the concept of desert to carry too heavy a burden. The concept of desert has great intrinsic appeal; no one wants a legal system in which the law metes out more punishment than the criminal deserves. But by importing other values into the concept, some desert theorists are playing into the strength of the traditionalist defenders of the prison. As seen in the next chapter, they should not be surprised if in many jurisdictions their efforts have unintended consequences. Winning the battle by securing desert as the basis for incarceration, they may lose the war: Conservatives in many states are successfully arguing that desert should mandate longer sentences and higher incarceration rates than under current practice. From our perspective, desert is extremely useful as a limiting principle for imprisonment; there is no guarantee that if we expand its role to that of a defining principle we shall like the definitions imposed upon us by superior political force. The trick will be to find a defining principle that is politically acceptable to both left and right as well as some consensus on its limiting principles. It is to that unenviable task that we now turn.

5 A Policy Proposal

Introduction

During the 1950s, a Jules Feiffer cartoon made sport of Dwight Eisenhower's effort to find a stance on school integration. "I'm against the extremists on both sides," the president was portrayed as saying. "I'm against those who want to blow up the schools, and against those who want to keep them open."

This was, of course, a false dilemma. The nation was not forced to choose between traditional unacceptable practices and a solution that was worse than the original problem. The same may be said of today's imprisonment debate; we are not forced to choose between a continuation of current practices and a policy that may make matters even worse. That is the effect, however, of limiting the options to the pure "Just build" and "Don't build" schools. In this chapter, we attempt to broaden this horizon. We present a policy package which develops some fundamental ideas and integrates them to cover sentencing, construction, and programs. The proposal presents a plan whereby, with the necessary political will, the institution of imprisonment could move from being simply a homeostatic system to one that operates on principles. Our package combines elements of liberal and conservative views, which are usually opposed to each other. It also combines elements of the debates on whether to build and on whom to imprison, which are usually considered separately. The crucial feature of our proposal is that it involves breaking down the fusion of punishment with prison which has for so long dominated American penal policy and practice.

We neither expect nor wish that this proposal will sweep the country. Necessarily presented in general terms, it cannot take account here of the regional and local variations that make any recommendation more or less acceptable. Certainly, the variations among state systems make impossible any uniform application. Our proposal does provide, however, a framework within which individual jurisdictions can relate the size and composition of prison populations to their living conditions and the services they receive. If the proposal influences one or two jurisdictions which share our dissatisfaction with the present and are seeking openings to a better future, the aim of this book will have been achieved.

We emphasize the links among the three components of sentencing, construction, and programs. It is obvious that sentencing policy affects population size and that this affects perceptions of how much construction is required. Less obvious is that the purposes sought by legislatures and sentencing judges will influence the services provided—or not provided—by correctional administrators. And sometimes obscured altogether is the fact that construction policy will often affect who goes to prison. To use current jargon, capacity affects both population size and composition. The need for a policy that is sensitive to these relations is a major theme of this book.

The contemporary policy problem can be related to our earlier discussion of colonial criminal justice. We noted that some critics have charged that prerevolutionary America lacked punishments in the middle range. Whether or not one agrees with that analysis of history, it is certainly an accurate description of America's predicament today. In large measure, imprisonment is overused because legislatures, prosecutors, and judges do not know what else to do. In particular, the lack of punishments that are not incarcerative but are still frankly punitive perpetuates by default the dominance of the prison. Legalist needs for retribution cannot now be met in other ways, so they have to be met by imprisonment. Thus the prison is forced to do the double duty of crime control and legalism, without any principles for striking the balance. A focus on the distinctive contribution of the prison to social order, and a practical concentration on that task, is the first step toward a rational and efficient policy.

What is special about prison? What can it clearly do that other punishments cannot? It can confine people. It can keep them, at least while they are inside, from repeating the behavior against the general society that put them there in the first place. To go beyond this distinctive function is to enter a morass. Early critics of the prison understood this. As William Eden noted as long ago as the eighteenth century, the contribution of the penitentiary to either general deterrence or legalism is problematic; it cannot, he maintained, "communicate the benefit of example, being in its nature secluded from the eye of the people."[1] The basis of a sensible policy is to ensure that the prison does what it can—immobilize criminals—and then to find other, acceptable measures for doing what it cannot.

The following analysis rests on a frankly subjective judgment about the seriousness of various types of crime. Prison is not the logical punishment for any particular offense; it can incapacitate check forgers as well as murderers. But as the most serious sanction available in almost all cases, its use can logically be concentrated on commensurately serious offenders. Moreover, it is a scarce political and economic resource, and such concentration is therefore reinforced by a decent respect for individual liberty and for the taxpayers' money. Those who do not distinguish degrees of seriousness among offenses, or who feel that some other kind of behavior is more serious than violent crime, will simply not be friendly to our plan. We should at least be clear that their disagreement is a matter of political and social values and not the result of some divination of the logic of imprisonment.

This fundamental premise can be integrated with two other principles in the following summary of our proposal. The three elements can then be expanded and defended in turn. (1) On sentencing, the dominant justifying aim of incarceration in a prison should be incapacitation. Imprisonment should be the punishment of choice, not for all offenses as it is under current practice but primarily where it seems necessary to meet the threat of physical violence. (2) On construction, new prison space should be built primarily to replace existing facilities or to bring them up to humane and constitutional standards. In most states, the effect of construction programs, indeed the condition of funding them, should be that they do not increase current capacity. (3) On programs, we recommend that administrators maintain those existing services and begin new ones that can be truly voluntary and facilitative. While there are dangers here, the alternatives are worse.

The need for a broad-gauged proposal can be demonstrated by a brief review of some other suggestions which do not go far toward a politically acceptable revision of penal policy.

Community Corrections

At least since the 1960s, a group of critics has argued for the replacement of traditional imprisonment with much less restrictive placement. While details of this idea are often cloudy, it usually involves a group-home or other low-security facility, and location in a residential or at least urban area rather than an isolated rural one. A review of the criminological literature of the past fifteen years would suggest that community corrections represents a major force in American penology. In fact, its prominence is largely rhetorical. After years of intellectual fashion for this idea, the federal survey found in 1978 that of half a million correctional inmates only 8,000 were in community corrections. Nor was this a result of lack of space. Most jurisdictions reported that they had empty community-based capacity,[2] although that does not keep the faithful from calling for more community corrections money and arguing that they have found the solution to prison crowding.

Why has community corrections not been adopted, or even seriously attempted, as the solution to the prison problem? In terms of our earlier discussion, it failed in several ways. First, community corrections as currently conceived simply does not meet the crime control requirements of a large-scale criminal justice policy. It is irrelevant to that substantial pool of serious violent offenders against whom society needs and demands substantial protection. Equally important, community corrections fails to meet the needs we have described as legalist. It concentrates so much on the interest of the inmates, and in reducing the incarcerated population, that it has become suspect from the perspective of the right and even the center of the political spectrum. In the context of the punishment-imprisonment fusion described above, most Americans would be suspicious of community corrections, regardless of what rhetoric accompanied it. Its proponents' excessive claims have only aggravated that suspicion. The result has been that American society has given a quite different meaning to the term "community corrections": the jail, and not the group home, has attracted most of the less-serious offenders. Traditional legalists may have captured community corrections as, in many states, they have captured sentencing reform. They have certainly made it impossible for community corrections to serve as the basis for a broader imprisonment strategy.

Reducing Sentences

A second proposal that cannot serve as the center of a solution to prison problems calls for a sweeping reduction in sentence length. We have shown that many critics, among them Eugene Doleschal of the influential National Council on Crime and Delinquency, maintained that American sentences are longer than those anywhere else in the world.[3] From this, some infer that the key to current difficulties lies simply in trimming the excess from the number of years served in American prisons.

There is a kernel of good sense in this proposal. Its authors are correct that the size of the inmate population is a product of the number of prison commitments and the length of time they stay. This is implicitly recognized in the manipulation of time served as a safety valve, sometimes wholesale, as in California during the late 1960s. When the population gets "too large," whatever that is taken to mean, prison stays mysteriously get shorter. However, in the population boom of the mid-1970s, the variable of time served was much the lesser partner of new commitments in accounting for population increases.[4] Similarly, in the relatively slower growth rate of the later

1970s, time served did not decline substantially; the rate of new commitments simply dropped. It seems, therefore, that manipulating sentence length, while it may be desirable from other points of view, does not hold major promise as a realistic answer to the problem of prison crowding.

The other points of view, of course, again constitute the tricky but determinative feature. The actual time served for most prison commitments—in the jargon, the median time to first release—is about two years. This means that a one-week cut in the average sentence would yield a 1 percent reduction in prison population. For a liberal who feels that the prison population is, say, double what it should be, a one-year cut in time served would be required. That would leave one year as the average stay for all crimes. Although there is no magic length of sentence any more than there is a magic population size, we doubt that a prison sentence of one year, lying at the margin of the traditional misdemeanor penalty, would satisfy either the legalists or the crime controllers even among today's new breed of liberals. There is far less promise in sentence length for major cuts in population size than many of the critics would have us believe.

The Dangerous Few, the Imprisonable Many, and the Privileged Others

Three other proposals that receive support in some quarters, but not much here, may be discussed under a common rubric. In our view, these proposals fail to provide the basis for a solution not so much in their fundamental suggestion as in their lack of guidelines for applying it. They may be labeled with some facetiousness but with a serious intent: finding the dangerous few, finding the imprisonable many, and finding the privileged others.

As shown in Chapter 1, the effort to base a policy on finding the dangerous few has been led by the NCCD. In 1973, it presented a "carefully studied distinction between dangerous and non-dangerous offenders." Two types of dangerous offenders were defined: "(1) the offender who has committed a serious crime against a person and shows a behavior pattern of persistent assaultiveness based on serious mental disturbances and (2) the offender deeply involved in organized crime." It was also said that, by using these criteria of dangerousness, "in any state *no more than one hundred* persons would have to be confined in a single maximum security institution."[5]

As a substantial proportion of those showing "a behavior pattern of persistent assaultiveness based on serious mental disturbances" would presumably find their way to mental hospitals, and as those "deeply involved in organized crime" are notoriously elusive and enjoy a high degree of impunity, this NCCD policy implied a problem not in construction but in disposing of surplus cell blocks. However, by 1977 their "carefully studied distinction" had undergone a substantial transformation. Dangerousness was redefined to cover "an act of violence, actual or threatened, or a felony carried out by members of organized crime syndicates. Using this classification NCCD would imprison the dangerous offender for terms that could be extended as long as thirty years."[6] This time it is notable that no estimate of the number of persons who would have to be confined was offered. It is just as well. The combination of a much broader base and a tolerance for very long sentences would without doubt create population dimensions quite unacceptable to the NCCD. The absence of more specific offense categories and sentence lengths would create serious space and ethical problems for this superficial proposal so much favored on the left.

On the right wing of the debate, the problem of finding the imprisonable many is equally severe. We are thinking here of statements like James Q. Wilson's—that a great deal of new prison space must be built because "society clearly wants its criminal laws enforced."[7] Which laws, against which offenses, and which ones require imprisonment? Does society, that amorphous collection, want its laws enforced for crime control reasons—for incapacitation, or deterrence, or both—or is this a traditional legalist argument that perpetuates the link between law enforcement and incarceration? The reason that such broad sentiments cannot be the basis for a prison policy is not that they do not make sense—that is a matter of political values—but that they provide no guidance about how much space is necessary, and how many commitments would result from applying their recommendations. One could imagine, under the principles set out by Wilson, a prison population half again as large as today's; one could also imagine a population five or ten times as great. We do not criticize Wilson and others for stopping where they did; we argue only that it is necessary to go further in search of a practical policy.

By the privileged others we refer to those offenders who are not normally punished by incarceration even though their crimes may be quite damaging to society. In general, these are white-collared, and white-skinned, criminals. The argument made currently by some blacks but principally by white liberals is that the racial balance of the inmate population must be changed. In an odd kind of equal protection argument, Wendell Bell and others maintain that incarceration must be used against more whites and fewer blacks.[8] This, they claim, will not only solve the prison crowding problem but will produce a fairer system and restore the faith of both whites and blacks in that fairness.

This is a large and difficult subject, one that would require a separate analysis if it were to be covered completely. But a few observations can be made. First, this proposal is largely indifferent to the purpose of crime control based on violence against the person. Second, it is not clear that such a course, once embarked upon and pursued with the kind of vigor that liberal ideologues recommend, would reduce the prison population at all. Indeed, it might have the opposite effect. If the traditional uses of the prison for personal and property crime were not to be replaced but merely supplemented by this new class of white offenders—of whom there are a much larger pool than of street criminals—this liberal solution might inflate the prison population by as much or more than its conservative counterpart. The attempt to find and incarcerate the privileged others perpetuates the link between punishment and prison. This is traditional on the right but surprising and (by its own lights) self-defeating on the left.

Policy Directions

We turn now to our own three-component policy package. The first component is the most difficult and unfashionable, and we might as well meet it head-on. As shown in Chapter 4, the literature of the past decade reflects a general trend toward desert as the primary justifying aim of incarceration. This trend has been driven by a well-founded skepticism about rehabilitative aspirations as guides to who should be imprisoned and how long they should stay. We share this skepticism and hold no brief for the notion of large-scale indeterminacy in sentencing, or for the ability of parole boards to assess an inmate's progress toward some chimerical goal. However, desert cannot provide the basis for a policy on whom to imprison in the first place.

The concept of desert is being asked to carry too heavy a burden. It cannot tell legislatures or sentencing judges who should go to prison and who should not. When it comes to choosing a punishment, there is nothing distinctive about imprisonment in the context of desert philosophy, any more than desert can specify the merits of whipping or probation. With the residual exception noted below, the general idea of desert provides no guidance in decisions about whether or not to imprison. For these purposes the concept is empty. Moreover, it may be "coopted," and turned against the very liberals who espouse it. Desert is already being used in some places to justify longer sentences. The surprise expressed at this by David Greenberg and Drew Humphries[9] is itself surprising; their dismay stems from the failure to anticipate the effects, in many jurisdictions, of differing notions not only of whether imprisonment is deserved but of how much imprisonment is deserved.

If, then, the currently fashionable notion of desert will not lead us to an imprisonment strategy, what will? We maintain that for the vast majority of cases the answer lies in the relatively unfashionable concept of incapacitation. Moreover, at the core of this answer lies the completely unfashionable notion of—dare we say it?—the prediction of future behavior. This seems to us the only legitimate primary basis for imprisonment. Rather than try to reimport it into a defining desert philosophy, it seems far preferable to acknowledge its central place, confront its possible risks, and see whether these cannot be addressed using desert as a limiting principle to ensure the humane and just treatment of those who are incapacitated.

The recent emphasis on individual desert has led some to forget that criminal punishments are routes to social order. A condition of this order is the minimization of both the reality and the fear of random physical violence. To minimize these forces of disorder is the primary goal of the criminal justice system. In the choice of sanctions, of course, routes to order must be sought that are consistent with competing values of individual liberty and fairness. But within those limits, the system should be obliged to do what it can—to use its resources efficiently—to preserve that order. In the absence of confidence about the marginal deterrent effects of any punishments, it seems prudent and fair to all concerned to do what can be done: to make it impossible, for some limited period of time, for violent criminals to commit new offenses against the general society.

The corollary is unpopular but inescapable: the decision to incapacitate a particular offender implies a judgment about his likely future behavior. The conventional criticism of this strategy is that the agents of society may be wrong about whether this offender will "do it again." In turn, many infer that this danger—known in the jargon as the problem of the false positive prediction—bars society from imprisoning anyone on this basis.

Federal Judge Macklin Fleming entitled a book *The Price of Perfect Justice*.[10] We wish that we had thought of that line first, because it epitomizes our reaction to the foregoing argument. In making the false positive the measure of imprisonment policy, liberals become their own enemies. They make the best the enemy of the better. To the extent, if any, that they reduce the likelihood of a violent offender going to prison, they act against the interests of precisely the body of minority poor they have appointed themselves to defend. And they force society, which is not about to abandon the prison altogether, to search for and find in desert a potentially more sweeping justification, which may result in the incarceration of more offenders for longer periods than is currently the case.

To get the benefits of the desert contribution without paying its excessive costs, one must understand its partial character. To ask for a single justification for both dimensions of imprisonment is to ask too much. The two key decisions in the process—whether and how long—must be distinguished, and they need not have the same rationale. Indeed, the distinct justifications for the decision to put someone in prison, and later for the decision to let him out, may even come into conflict. At that point, judgment becomes crucial, and special care for the rights of the individual offender must be taken. But this is hardly an argument for reliance on a single justification.

Even if incapacitation is accepted as the primary justification for the decision to imprison, there remains a small residual need for a supplementary use. In the Model Penal Code and elsewhere,[11] this is called the depreciation of the seriousness of the offense. For example, in Morris's witty case of the wife murderer with no plans to remarry—more seriously, in cases where incapacitation is not the justification for imprisonment because there is no fear of a repetition of the offense—it might still be necessary to imprison some small number of additional offenders. There is an obvious need for this action in cases of extremely serious crimes, and also for exemplary sentences in such instances as the most outrageous cases of tax evasion. The primary reason for such imprisonment is that people would otherwise believe that justice had not been done and that the violation of social norms had not been accorded its proper importance.

This residual justification must remain small, and even then it is subject to abuse. It makes a bow to precisely the fusion of punishment and imprisonment that we are trying to break. So long as a sizable number of citizens believe that a sizable number of offenses go unpunished unless someone is locked up, the problem of a rational imprisonment strategy will remain difficult. On the other hand, it would be unrealistic and naive to deny that this attitude will to some extent remain a feature of the American political landscape. Some narrow band must remain, at the top of the punishment scale, containing penalties that can be invoked for largely symbolic reasons. Since we oppose capital punishment in this or any other context, ritual or legalist imprisonment seems the inescapable alternative.

Incapacitation gives us a defining principle, but does not by itself tell us how many people will or should be locked up. This cannot be done by abstract categories, as our analysis of the NCCD position has shown. The size of the class of offenders violent enough to be imprisoned will be influenced by the number and nature of the choices in any particular case. Moreover, these choices must be spelled out in considerably more detail than is usual in attempts to limit the use of imprisonment. The great weakness of such efforts is not that they are not based on good ideas but that these good ideas are not taken far enough. Neither a legislator, a sentencing judge, nor a private citizen can make an intelligent choice among the abstractions of "prison" and "probation" and "work release." It is what happens in each case that determines one's preferences.

The failure of the prison's critics has been their assumption that general pronouncements about alternatives will affect practice. Many of these critics remain puzzled and angry about the failure of these alternatives to take hold on a large scale. But this failure will continue so long as skeptics are unable to determine to what extent these alternatives really meet their requirements. This is especially true concerning retributivist sentiments and demands that the seriousness of the offense not be depreciated. Only when alternatives can be specified sufficiently to satisfy this demand will fewer people have to meet it by going to prison. People around the country will differ legitimately on the application of our general principles to particular cases, making this a task for individual jurisdictions rather than a book on policy directions. But the homework must be done before the prison's critics will make progress.

Some general guidance can be offered here. A tangible relation between the nonincarcerative but still punitive sanction, and the offense it punishes, is a good place to start. This is especially true of nonviolent property crimes; these represent the largest category of offenses which are imprisonable under current practice but not under our plan. Today's policies make the worst of at least three worlds. In many cases, they enhance the risk that too light a sanction will be imposed, because prison seems to the sentencing judge too severe for the particular circumstances. In other cases, they result in the imposition of a sanction which *is* too severe. And in both cases they accomplish nothing, except possibly provide some symbolic satisfaction for vengeful feelings on the part of the victim. The requirement for restitution to the victim of property crimes, perhaps "with interest" for the fear and anxiety involved, is a good basis for an avowedly retributive legalist sanction. It can be backed up with the threat of incarceration if the offender does not meet his court-imposed obligation. But the shift of prison and jail from first to second or third resort is a major, salutary change. It begins with the creation and calibration of punishments with real content that lie between "nothing" and "prison."

Limitations on the offender's leisure, but short of total withdrawal of his liberty, constitute a parallel category. These might be related to, and used as punishment for, whatever the particular community defines as violations of public order and social norms as well as for some property crimes and minor crimes against the person. The variation in these offense categories is tremendous, both over time in

American history and across jurisdictions today. But they have in common the notion that the offender has done something with his free time which unacceptably disrupts the community. A proportionate withdrawal of some of that free time makes sense as a sanction. Already, in some American jurisdictions, judges are experimenting with house arrest for this purpose. Other countries, such as Sweden, are using existing incarcerative facilities. In large, dense American cities, frequent-furlough jail sentences, perhaps emphasizing evenings or weekends to minimize the interrupting of employment, may be necessary. In smaller communities or tighter neighborhoods, house arrest may be quite feasible.

Public service, not to a specific victim but to the community as a whole, may be another option. Judges in juvenile courts have always used this in specific circumstances; at the lower range of adult seriousness it has promise as well. Severe fiscal penalties paid to the public treasury may be still another alternative. But we do not want to pitch our general argument—the need for punishments with real content short of imprisonment—on our own specific examples. Once the need for such a calibration is widely recognized, individual communities will be imaginative in applying their own mores to the particular circumstances of an offense. Legalism and localism go hand in hand.

We offer also some general guidance on drawing the line between new nonincarcerative sanctions and traditional ones. Who should go to prison? For whom is the distinctively incarcerative function the sensible punishment of choice? Murderers combine the two justifications of crime control and legalism; the most serious crime demands and therefore deserves the most serious sanction, a status to which we have promoted imprisonment. There may be exceptions to this rule—such as a fight issuing in an apparently accidental but marginally culpable death—but such examples will be few.

Firearm robbery represents another clear case in its most serious forms. The danger to society is sufficient to prevent early repetitions of thefts with loaded guns, and those involving physical injury or serious endangerment. Even for first adult convictions, we recommend incarceration as the appropriate sanction in the vast majority of cases. Exceptions will occur, and these can be determined only by the mitigating circumstances of the individual case. A similar line can be drawn in the amorphous category of assault. For nonrobbery assaults which do not involve firearms or injury, we would require a showing of repetitiveness or aggravating seriousness before recommending imprisonment as the punishment of choice. But where these conditions are met, imprisonment even for first convictions will be justified in most cases.

The two remaining major components of today's prison population are burglary and drug offenses. These can be discussed together. Both present difficulties of generalization, since they mean different things in different jurisdictions. But both require a line drawn between professionalism and amateurism. This line may sometimes be hard to draw in a particular case; it must be drawn nevertheless. We recommend incarceration for professionals and a bias for non-incarcerative but punitive alternatives in the case of amateurs. The legalist need must be served here, but the prison is not necessary to serve it. The careerist pattern, however, should be proved by experience and not merely attributed. Thus incarceration should be applied only to second adult convictions (except in rare cases), as distinct from loaded-gun robbery where a first adult conviction would be sufficient.

The second crucial decision to be made is when to let the offender out. Our prescription of a desert limit to the length of sentence is not self-defining. There is, however, a further clue in the age distribution of offenses. With the peak offense rates for imprisonable crimes concentrated in the late teens and early twenties, the first year of a prison sentence prevents far more crimes than the tenth year. This means that in crime prevention yield, an incapacitation strategy—especially in the real world of limited correctional resources—is most efficient if it concentrates on ensuring that all who qualify are locked up at least for some time. That may mean shorter average stays than some people would like. But to the extent that very long sentences are a feature of today's practices, they are very inefficient in controlling the number of offenses. Moreover, these long sentences in most cases violate the desert limit, which we have argued is an important part of meeting the demands of the revisionist legalists on the left-center of the political spectrum.

How long is long enough to maximize the incapacitative gains and yet not exceed the desert limit? We suggest five years, as a maximum. This is controversial; to many on the right there is something very satisfying about the broad option of throwing the key away, and on the left we have seen an acceptance in some quarters for time served as long as thirty years. But we need not repeat the costs in inefficient incapacitation, violations of fairness, and excessive prison populations and budgets. The satisfaction that comes from the option of throwing the key away, or even the reality of it in a small number of cases, is empty. It makes harder, not easier, the use of prison as it should be used: to limit directly the amount of crime we would otherwise have.

There must be room for exceptions to our proposed five-year limit. Neither this system nor any other will operate by remote control. In some instances time served will have to be longer, indeed span most of an offender's life, to avoid depreciating the seriousness of the offense; all of us would be offended by Charles Manson's release after only five years in prison. Another possible exception is the case where a diagnosis of psychosis or other mental disorder creating real and continuing physical danger has been made and repeatedly re-affirmed. These cases are subject to abuse, and every effort must be made to restrain the abuses. But the occasional public abuse, which occurs despite everyone's best efforts, is not an argument against an entire social policy. Once that is understood, and not until then, we shall have made some progress toward a rational policy on imprisonment.

Since this chapter strives for policy directions rather than a detailed penal code, we resist the temptation to specify sentence lengths for particular offenses. These are properly the task of legislators, judges, prosecutors, and other officials who can reflect regional and local mores. Nor do we attempt a forecast of the number of prisoners that would follow from the application of our general principles. This would be both presumptuous by overriding local values, and misleading by conveying a spurious precision. We shall show, however, that our sentencing principles are consistent with a concern for the link between construction policy and population size.

By our standards of imprisonable crimes, we find a great deal more flexibility in the prison system than is generally acknowledged. The standard conservative view is that the prisons are already bulging, and any effort toward greater severity—which ours certainly is for some offenses—requires massive expansions in capacity. But if the threshold is moved and the priorities we have recommended are accepted, the problem is by no means intractable. Of all the prison inmates in the country, only about 47 percent have been sent there for crimes against the person: homicide, arson, rape, robbery, and assault.[12] Over one-third are there for property crimes, principally burglary and auto theft. The remainder, about 20 percent, have been convicted of crimes against public order, most of which are drug offenses. A breakdown by region makes this even clearer, as shown in table 5.1.

These data show that a substantial fraction of people now incarcerated would not be imprisoned under our proposed principles. If the nonviolent offenders were not imprisoned, a great deal of correctional capacity would become available either for longer stays for violent offenders now incarcerated, or to lock up many violent criminals who now go free. In either case, or in any sensible combination of them, additional capacity can be provided for violent offenders without huge capital outlays. This will free construction budgets to do what they should be doing—improving conditions—by clarifying in

Table 5.1
1978 Percentage Distribution of the State Prison Inmates by Region, by Offense Type

Region	Crimes against the Person	Crimes against Property	Crimes against Public Order
Northeast	45	37	18
North Central	52	34	14
South	44	41	15
West	48	28	24
U.S. total	47	37	16

SOURCE: Abt Associates data from "Survey of State and Federal Adult Correctional Facilities," unpublished.
NOTE: Figures rounded to nearest whole number.

advance that they are barred from the open-ended and irrational building programs of the past.

The place of existing capacity in a comprehensive construction strategy is analogous to the place of desert in sentencing: it cannot tell us what to do but it can tell us what not to do. Both cases provide a necessary sense of limits, both seek to prevent traditional abuses. In construction policy, the limits reflect a sensitivity to the danger that new capacity invites new populations. As a rule, the principle tells us not to exceed existing capacity. There will again be exceptions, particularly where judicial intervention and slow innovation mean new capacity must be built before old facilities are phased out. But in most jurisdictions, there is enough acceptable capacity now to apply our plan for sentencing, both on who goes to prison and for how long.

There are some jurisdictions which are already using existing capacity as the principle of selection for at least who goes to prison. This is a difficult matter to assess. It does limit the use of a sanction which we regard as grossly overused. But in some of these instances, this is hardly a principled limitation. It does not address directly the question of the composition of the prison population; it merely controls its size. While over time this will surely have broad effects on composition, one can hardly have confidence that these effects will be in desired directions.

In a state such as Illinois, which already concentrates heavily on incapacitation as a justifying aim, a ceiling of this kind may be desirable.[13] However, other jurisdictions which manipulate release policy according to demands of capacity and litigation may not yield such acceptable results. If they currently use the prison as a catch-all, their imprisonment policy may become even more unprincipled; this is often the effect of many efforts to limit the population size without other guiding ideals. Thus a normative policy cannot be based on purely quantitative considerations. But as desert limits sentence length, so existing capacity can and should in most cases limit the use of construction budgets. There is enough to do with the money that must be spent to improve conditions. In many instances, an insistence on this goal will yield a construction policy that reduces rather than expands capacity. A holding to the consensus standard of sixty square feet per inmate would have that effect in almost all jurisdictions.

Adapting Today's Practices

In order to relate a sentencing policy to the issue of capacity requirements, we must subject the reader to some detail on at least one jurisdiction. We have selected New York, using the 1977/78 data that were the latest available;[14] more recent provisional data do not undermine the following analysis and may in fact strengthen it.

In an average month's business in the New York courts about ninety persons are found guilty of homicide. Eighty of these offenders are sentenced to state or local prisons for terms ranging from six months to life (4% of the sentences are under one year). The remaining ten are sentenced to probation or given a conditional discharge. During the same month, sixty-three persons will be sentenced for felonious sexual assault, including rape. Of these, nineteen will be placed on probation and another two or three will get conditional discharges. Of the 66 percent who do time, one-fifth will serve less than a year.

When one considers sentencing practice in New York for the several classes of felony, the remarkable feature of the data is the evident lack of discrimination among offenses. Sexual assault (66% to prison) and drug offenses (67%) are treated almost alike. Robbery, which involves violence or the threat of violence, and burglary, which generally does not, differ by only 20 percent, and the probability of incarceration for robbery is only nine percentage points lower than that for homicide. In New York City, courts appear even less sensitive to the nature of the offense: 80.6 percent of robbers, 74.2 percent of burglars, and 75.9 percent of drug offenders go to state or city prison.

The amount of time served by those in prison is similarly unrelated to the offense. Figure 5.1 shows the median number of months that state prisoners served prior to release in 1975. The shortest of these times (20.1 months for burglary) is about a third less than the longest (29.7 months for negligent or willful homicide). The offenses which make up the greatest bulk of the felony caseload (robbery, burglary, and drugs) have medians falling within a comparatively narrow range

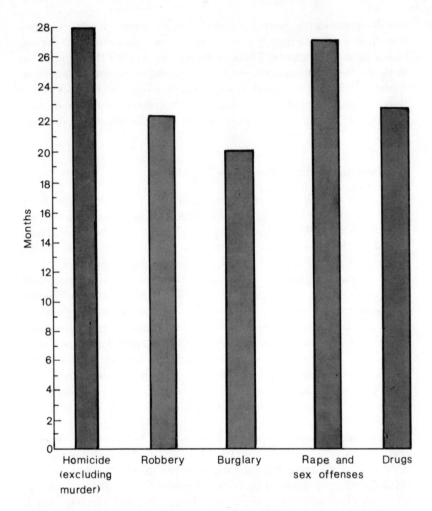

FIGURE 5.1: Median time to first release from New York State prisons (1975). Source: New York State Department of Corrections, *Annual Report, 1977*.

of about three months, although both laymen and criminologists tend to think of these offenses as differing greatly in seriousness.

Suppose we adopted a more discriminating set of sanctions—one in which serious violent offenders were significantly more likely to go to prison than property criminals, who in turn were treated as severely as drug cases, and one in which length of prison terms also bore some proportionate relationship to the seriousness of the harm done. What would be the consequence in the courts and prisons of the state?

For the sake of concreteness, let us take a hypothetical example that could not be precisely reflected in actual practice but still gives some sense of scale. Assume that the distribution of offenses remains approximately as it was in 1977 but that every person convicted of homicide, kidnapping, and arson, 90 percent of those convicted of rape, 80 percent of those convicted of robbery, 50 percent of those convicted of felonious assault, and 25 percent of those convicted of illegal possession of dangerous weapons were given a prison term. As of 1975 just under 70 percent of New York State prison inmates had been convicted of one of these offenses. Under these circumstances, these kinds of results are still well under New York's current prison capacity and would leave prison space available for persistent burglars and the sellers of hard drugs.

The logic of differentiated sentencing has two sides: if sanctions become harsher for those convicted of crimes against the person, they can also become more lenient for property and public order offenders. Although the chances of incarceration are about the same for violent offenders as for other felons, the violent criminal is more likely to go to a state institution, while a comparatively larger fraction of burglars and thieves stay at local institutions, where sentences are generally shorter but less comfortable.

Let us continue our hypothetical calculation of effects by supposing (1) only half as many sentences requiring incarceration are given for nonviolent crimes, (2) local correctional institutions continue as the primary sanction for these offenses, and (3) prison terms for those who do go to state institutions are cut in half. Under these assumptions a sharply reduced number of burglary convictions and of drug convictions would result in sentences to state prison, and, of the 25 percent of prison beds now occupied by nonviolent felons, a substantial proportion would be emptied.

These hypothetical sanction levels have not been selected arbitrarily. A sentencing system which followed the assumptions listed above would have virtually no effect on the total number of inmates, and hence to first approximation, none of the disruptive cost implications associated with the one-sided "Get tough" plans advocated by some. These are not the only sanction levels with this property; there are infinitely many possible adjustments which remain cost-neutral. These were chosen only as a simple expression of a desire for more nearly proportionate punishment. But we chose New York because it shows the flexibility even in a system that is already relatively advanced toward an incapacitative emphasis. In many other states with large prison populations, our argument has even greater force; this is especially true of the South.

The conventional wisdom is that, as a region, the South's correctional problems are worse than anywhere else in the country. This is probably true in some respects, untrue in many others. But here the important point is that the South has a larger fraction of nonviolent inmates than do the other regions.[15] For our purposes, this creates a potential flexibility that others do not have; it would be possible, without excessive risks to public safety and without increasing the population or the capacity of the system, to adopt the principles we recommend. The South is commonly regarded as the most intractable region, with its prisons bulging and its administrators in litigation. But it may paradoxically be our most promising ground for major population reductions with low crime control costs.

The flexibility that already exists in the system is already being recognized in some parts of the South and elsewhere. In Alabama, for example, a federal judge imposed a population ceiling based on capacity constraints and then sought outside advice about the prospects of reclassifying the security requirements of the individual inmates.[16] The recommended downward shift would allow up to one-third of the prisoners to be moved to lower classifications, and a substantial fraction to be decarcerated altogether. In New York as well, even with its relatively greater emphasis on incapacitation, officials are using narrower definitions of dangerousness to make more inmates eligible for the lower security facilities, where most vacancies occur.

It may be objected that the forcing of reclassification by capacity constraints is a reversion to a head-counting incarceration policy rather than a principled one. We cannot agree. Once a decision has been made on grounds of incapacitation that an offender does require imprisonment, it does not follow that he must necessarily be locked up in the most restrictive and severe conditions available. Even under current practice, it is well recognized that the system over-classifies as a matter of routine. We feel, for example, that regarding burglary first imprisonments where there have been no jail-escape attempts or other aggravating circumstances, the guiding principle should be a bias for the low side of the security spectrum rather than the high side. There are risks, but they are acceptable, especially when balanced by the risks of unnecessary damage to less-serious offenders placed in excessively severe confinement. The reflexive equation of all imprisonment with the fortress megaprison is simply a variation on the fusion of punishment with prison which we are trying to erode. It is legitimate and principled to use the constraint of capacity to accelerate that erosion. Forcing a redefinition of the requirements of incapacitation is only one tactic in this overall strategy.

The link to correctional programs of our other two principles must also be indicated. Clearly, our incapacitative emphasis is consistent with the call of Morris and others for the abandonment of rehabilitation as the justifying purpose of imprisonment.[17] Also, we support his further plea for the expansion of those programs that can be truly voluntary and facilitative.[18] This view is generally defended on grounds of human dignity[19] and fundamental rights of citizenship.[20] But it can be more directly linked to our policy on sentencing.

An imprisonment policy that concentrates on incapacitation must acknowledge its roots in judgments about future behavior and the virtual certainty that some of those judgments will be wrong. We have argued that the problem of some false positives does not swamp the societal risks of a much larger number of false negatives. But this calculation imposes upon officials a heavy obligation to treat everyone incarcerated as well as possible within the limits of budgets and security. The inmates are obviously in some kind of need; otherwise they would not have committed crimes in the first place. The need may be skills, job contacts, counseling—and the list is of course much longer. On moral grounds, the attack on social service as a justification for imprisonment *increases* the requirement to provide human services after incarceration. Incapacitative emphasis should have the paradoxical effect of strengthening the human service role in contemporary corrections.

Thus what is often bemoaned as the end of the rehabilitative ideal can and should be the basis for a new beginning. It rests not only on general rights but also on specific obligations created by a new purpose for the institution of imprisonment. Our strategy tries to liberate correctional human service by asking it to do only what it can, and by relieving it of any responsibility for public safety. If conducted in that spirit it may make some contribution to public safety as well, but that is not the reason for doing it. The goals of incapacitation and correctional programs, commonly throught to be in bitter competition, can be closely linked. Implementation of this recognition should strengthen the institution once its primary focus is changed. The advocates of correctional rehabilitation should find this acceptable.

A specific implication shifts the locus of deciding what services to provide from the administrator or the social worker to the prisoner himself. To resist this is to remain wedded to a coercive rather than a facilitative view of correctional programs. Furthermore, resistance means that the incapacitative emphasis of the institution itself has not really been accepted. Old attitudes die hard, but officials will have to anticipate that most of the services requested will be oriented not to the inner life of the prison but to life outside it. Contact visits, truly useful skills, and expanded use of work release are only examples. The catalogue will be expanded further when officials learn another lesson they may reflexively resist: prisoners must be asked what they believe would help them. Traditional resistance on the right has been accompanied, as in Milton Rector's statement that "our moral obligation is to act in accordance with our belief, not to distribute questionnaires,"[21] by an arrogance on the left. But from our perspective, correctional administrators and prison reformers *should* be in the business of distributing questionnaires. Moreover, these must be distributed not in the academy but in the prison yards.

Conclusion: A Sense of Limit

In this book's opening paragraph, we argued that the time is opportune for attempting significant change in American penal policy. We have made a proposal that tries to capitalize on that opportunity. However, it is important not to exaggerate either the prospects for change or the benefits from the acceptance of our plan. Claiming too much will be as bad as missing the opportunity altogether. An unfounded optimism is not only unrealistic; it may be positively dangerous. There is support for this fear in the history we have described; it is at periods of the most excessive claims that the greatest indignities have been wrought by the institutions of imprisonment. A sense of limit about our proposal will help its authors and anyone who tries to apply it.

The first risk is in claiming too much for the crime control that would result from our strategy. In recent years some analysts have made excessive estimates of the offense reductions that could flow from an incapacitative emphasis. Shinnar and Shinnar, for example, seem to suggest that if every person convicted of a violent crime were imprisoned for five years the rate of violent crimes could be reduced by as much as 80 percent.[22]

A more sensible attempt has been made by Petersilia and Greenwood. In their study, an attempt was made to estimate the effect mandatory minimum prison sentences would have on adult crime rates by analyzing data on a random sample of defendants convicted of serious offenses over a two-year period in the Denver, Colorado, District Courts. The technique they employed involved using career histories to estimate the probable incapacitation effects if offenders had been sentenced differently in the past. The procedure involved taking a cohort of arrested or convicted offenders, examining their past convictions, and determining whether each offender would have been imprisoned at the time of his current offense if a particular sentencing policy had been applied at the time of his last conviction.[23]

For the present purpose it is sufficient to consider their findings in relation to the impact of incapacitation strategies on violent crime: violent criminals being defined in this context as offenders charged with robbery, rape, aggravated assault, homicide, and kidnapping. Petersilia and Greenwood estimated the extent to which the violent cohort's crimes would have been prevented by the imposition of mandatory prison sentences for their preceding adult felony conviction under a variety of different sentencing policies.[24]

They found that only a severely stringent policy, under which every offender convicted of any adult felony, violent or not, regardless of prior record, were sentenced to a mandatory prison term of five years, might lessen violent crime by one-third. This policy incidentally would increase prison population by close to 450 percent.[25]

A sentencing policy which would impose a five-year sentence for any person previously convicted of at least one adult felony would have prevented 16.0 percent of violent crimes and increased prison population by 190 percent. A sentencing policy requiring offenders to have prior convictions for violent offenses would have reduced violent crime by less than 7 percent, even with mandatory five-year sentences.[26]

This study shows graphically that long sentences have undramatic incapacitation benefits with unthinkable prison population costs. Certainly, in a system like Denver's, the marginal benefit of the further use of incapacitative sentences for serious violent offenses is much smaller than we have been led to expect. Of course one reason why further selective incapacitation of violent offenders yields modest benefits is that we already incapacitate substantial numbers of such offenders.

On the other hand, a priority policy of prison after first conviction for violent offenders would have a much more dramatic effect on the number of crimes occurring if our target offenders were not locked up at all. That is no mean feat in a system which is currently having a great deal of trouble doing anything right. And if the clearer focus of this sanction gives rise to a sensible range of alternatives, the crime control contribution of the total system may be further increased.

It is at this juncture that the "heroic restraint" of Beaumont and de Tocqueville in claiming solutions will serve us well. Indeed, some writers who have supported our plea for an incapacitative emphasis have done the cause a disservice by claiming too much for it. There is no sweeping solution to the crime problem here, or anywhere else in the criminal justice system of a democracy. Even concerning the effects of a plan limited to penal policy, there is simply too much we do not know. The crime reductions flowing from incapacitation may be larger than we hope for or smaller than we fear, depending upon how much additional deterrence is achieved. The offset from crimes committed by those who would be let out under our plan is another uncertainty. Offenses are not perfectly specialized; some offenders currently incarcerated for property crimes will undoubtedly commit crimes against the person if they are free to do so. No one knows how often such crime switching will occur with anything nearing precision. It seems fair to anticipate, however, that even if the absolute amount of crime were to increase marginally its composition might be influenced in the way we prefer. Our entire proposal rests on a judgment that violent crime against the person is the most serious in our society, is the proper primary concern of the criminal justice system, and will be reduced significantly if unmeasurably by the imprisonment strategy we propose.

Thus, without making excessive claims for crime reduction, we believe the plan is a fair meshing of liberal and conservative concerns. For the left, it would reduce the number of people who are imprisoned, improve the conditions under which they are held, place efforts at human services in as facilitative a setting as possible, and break the cycle of self-filling facilities where this process currently exists. For the right, it would raise the probability that all convicted criminals will receive some kind of punishment, will place more types of offenders under some form of formal social control, might affect the composition of crime in ways that reduce its social corrosiveness, and responds to the legalist call to have the law enforced. Some on each wing will feel that it does not go far enough; but as we have shown, that is precisely the kind of thinking that has precluded both consensus and change thus far.

Another constraint on our proposal stems quite properly from the diffuse character of the criminal justice system itself. We have resisted the temptation, and so should others, to bolster our structure with efforts to mandate sentences or eliminate plea bargaining. For our purposes, such efforts are either fruitless or misguided. Judges and prosecutors will and should retain extensive discretion over when and how to apply policy guidelines. To the extent that we have not persuaded them, search-and-destroy attacks on their discretion will probably not add a great deal. In Franklin Zimring's words, messages and not mandates are contained in our proposal. This is not the place to write a new code of criminal procedure.

A third limit on both the acceptability and effectiveness of our proposal stems from the sensitive matter of race. For reasons described above, the concentration of incapacitation of violent offenders will raise even further the already high disproportion of minority groups in the inmate population. This seems to us both an acceptable and desirable cost for a plan which, after all, benefits the broader minority population that is disproportionately victimized by violent crime. Beyond a general incapacitative emphasis, it will be aggravated by increased attention to the plight in specific cases of minority versus minority crimes.[27] But we recognize that, in the policymaking community which is overwhelmingly white, this implication may impose a major limit. We believe it to be misguided, but there it is.

Yet another obstacle may lie in the correctional bureaucracy. While in many jurisdictions our plan would affect the composition of the inmate population but not the size, in others it would probably reduce the absolute number of inmates. Where such reductions were substantial, one could anticipate opposition from guards unions and even from higher level bureaucrats. But surely the argument for a principled policy cannot be much weakened by this; on the contrary, to the extent that it is correct, it supports the view that inmate populations are inflated by considerations that have no place in an enlightened society. We can acknowledge the force of bureaucratic politics without making it the touchstone of our policy.

Fifth, under our proposal total correctional expenditure will increase, although imprisonment's share of the correctional budget will decline. An increase in correctional expenditure is foreordained by any program which increases the number of citizens subject to social control. However, the nature of investment in alternative forms of punitive social control differs fundamentally from expenditure on prison construction. There are no huge capital costs with long-range implications for capacity and thus for prison population. There can be flexibility in building design and utilization, and this flexibility will create opportunities to expand or contract facilities with relatively short lead times. To use a current bureaucratic cliche, there are advantages to be obtained from putting some of our institutions of punishment on a "soft money" budget. That is something we cannot do with the American megaprison.

Two other problems may be allowed to exhaust our candor. Under our proposal, some people who now go to jail may be forced to go to prison. This may occur, for example, in jurisdictions where violent crimes between members of minority groups are currently treated more leniently than similar interracial crimes. To the extent that this practice, ultimately racist in conception, plays a part, the flexibility in prison space may be less than it appears. However, a counterargument is equally plausible. An abandonment of both the link between punishment and incarceration, and also of the notion that the process itself is the punishment, could free a whole pool of new space now taken up by the jail. Even more than many prisons, jails would require extensive expenditure to raise facilities to adequate standards. (This is an argument for adopting a current-capacity limit on jail population as well.) But it is conceivable that our proposal can provide the basis for a broad reshaping of the entire institution of incarceration that will affect both prisons and jails. This book takes a first step toward that long-deferred day.

The discussion of jails mirrors and epitomizes our position on prisons. The core of contemporary difficulties is the weight and power of the traditional American fusion of punishment and incarceration. Keep it, and relatively little progress can be made. Break it, and all sorts of possibilities appear. The notion will die hard. Its strength is reflected in the language, whose importance we have stressed throughout; Americans make the word "convict" cover both an assessment of guilt and a person locked up. But while the weight of the past is considerable, it cannot be allowed to swamp the policy choices which ultimately determine the future.

6 The Cloudy Crystal Ball

This book has stressed the influence on penal policy of ideas and the people who specialize in them. From such an emphasis, we have drawn a somewhat more optimistic view of the future than is found in many other places. We acknowledge, however, that our focus may distort the larger picture; it would be easy to be led astray by concentrating on what people say they believe, and this concluding chapter attempts a balanced summary of both the opportunities and dangers that make up the nation's correctional prospects.

If our optimism is misplaced, incidentally, we shall at least join the ranks of otherwise astute observers who have been "wrong together" in the past. In one instance, Ives, the Edwardian historian, had a quite modern sarcasm about others' hopes for rehabilitation: "The broken-down, the cretinous, the neurotic, the unbalanced, once made to think, were somehow to solve all the terrific problems of disease and environment; repent, and so save themselves."[1] But when he came to offer his own prediction about the broad future of corrections, the result appears a little silly: "In the future there will be no ordinary crime. This I predict with quiet confidence. Calamities indeed will ever come;... a certain amount of madness and disease, and perhaps smouldering Berserk outbreaks of individual jealousy and hatred. These will be with us to the end of time, but prison populations will have passed away!"[2]

Even Beaumont and Tocqueville must take their lumps as correctional futurists. George Wilson Pierson wrote in the 1930s that "as embryo statesmen it was their pleasure, as self-conscious humanitarians their solemn duty, to translate experience into counsel and intuition into warning.... [It] became part of their literary routine to study the future, and to prophesy." But as Pierson acknowledges, "In their prison investigations...they were a long way from suspecting the changes that time would bring. In fact, ...could the two friends have had a true vision of the future, could someone have told them exactly what was to happen to the penitentiary question in the United States...they would have been stunned, incredulous, and more than a little angry."[3]

Pierson refers, of course, to the disillusion and abandonment of the great hopes and ideals of the early and mid-nineteenth century. In the twentieth century, he says, Tocqueville would have found in American prisons "no solitude, no silence, no penitence, no reform . . . this monument to American hope and philanthropy, given up to sheer housing."[4] But with the clarity of our hindsight and another century and a half of penal history, these disappointed expectations may clarify the twin possibilities of the current juncture.

It is tempting to make Pierson's summary the basis of future policy, and many contemporary critics are doing exactly this. Imprisonment will never be more than sheer housing, they say, so the nation had best admit it and abandon the hypocritical cant about rehabilitation. This view is shared by many in both liberal and conservative camps. The former say that the social service ideal is dangerous because it leads to incarceration of more and more citizens in the misguided belief that they will come out of prison better men than when they entered; the latter say that social service is not the purpose of the prison and that it only misleads the public and hampers the correctional administrator to saddle the system with some impossible goal. This coalition creates the attractive possibility that prison can be increasingly used for its correct purpose—incapacitation of dangerous offenders—but it also creates the risk that an important humanizing constraint on the system may be removed.

In late nineteenth-century England, the widespread abandonment of even the nominal ideal of rehabilitation contributed to a prison system that in Fox's words was "a living death." In our view, just as desert cannot be a defining principle for imprisonment but must remain a limiting one, the same is true of social service. The defining purpose of imprisonment—the reason for which society locks up a convicted criminal—should in most cases be incapacitation. But the rehabilitative ideal must constrain the punishment inflicted on the offender. It must remain part of the complex of correctional goals to allow and encourage convicts to emerge if not better men, at least not worse ones. The British example reminds us that, if America chooses a future for its prisons that is purely punitive, the effect of reaching the current crossroad may be to make the system more inhumane rather than to improve it.

Although the practical outcome of the current debate is by no means clear—and in any case, there will be no uniform outcome—the nation is certainly better off than when Pierson wrote, "Nowhere can one find any slightest excuse for optimism."[5] In Ignatieff's words, "Something fundamental is beginning to happen."[6] But that something could turn out to be either (as Rothman has predicted) "the beginning of the end of the total institution," or a reformulation of its purposes whose legacy is an even more enduring and punitive system, or a narrowing of its focus such as we have proposed, or any of a number of possibilities not examined here. To assume that the next task is merely a kind of intellectual mopping up would be a serious mistake. Indeed, the predicament of today's best reformers may be similar to that of their counterparts in the late eighteenth century; the parallel is worth pursuing.

Ignatieff has shown that the timing of an idea can be crucial to its success or failure. "Had Howard's *State of the Prisons* been published at any other time," he writes, "figures outside the small circle of reforming Dissenters might have been disposed to dismiss it as a worthy but tedious tract. Instead, it appeared at a moment of acute crisis in the administration of criminal justice."[7] However, the same historian has also demonstrated that "since there does not seem to have been any very noticeable outcry against prison abuses or physical punishments prior to the reform movement itself, it appears that the reformers took their own heightened sensitivity . . . as symptomatic of general social feeling."[8] Taking these two conditions together, one can understand not only why the eighteenth-century reformers' ideas did have an effect but also why their aims were garbled and distorted in the process. Many observers have noted that most systems in both America and England adopted part of Howard's scheme, notably the single cell ideal, and threw the rest away.

Contemporary reformers, especially on the left, would do well to take the story of Howard as a cautionary tale. They tend to argue as if the merits of their own proposals (especially of the construction moratorium) were accepted by all serious analysts and what remains is a tactical political battle for their acceptance. However, just as there was no outcry against prison conditions before the reformers started in the eighteenth century, so today there is no consensus in the general public either that prison conditions are too harsh or that incarceration is being overused. Concerning correctional conditions, Romilly's advice to Bentham still applies: the public "does not care tuppence" about prison conditions. Concerning the rate of incarceration, most Americans indicate in surveys a desire for harsher penalties, not more lenient ones. Although we have stressed the difficulty of translating this sentiment into detailed policy prescriptions, it does suggest that reformers had better think twice before they throw some of their suggestions into the public hopper. Their experience with the conservatives' co-opting of determinate sentencing, noted in Chapter 5, is otherwise likely to be repeated.

In the late twentieth century as in the late eighteenth, reformers run the risk that their efforts will backfire. Now as then, there exists a specialized, vocal, and fortunately influential reform constituency drawn from the legal, academic, and correctional administrative fields. They have an opportunity to humanize the practices of a social institution which, by all accounts, are pretty awful in too many places. But a partial success might be worse than nothing. In the eighteenth century, the defense of the rehabilitative ideal was used to justify increased incarceration in what turned out to be unreformed conditions. In the twentieth century, the attack on the rehabilitative ideal can be used to support practices which, in the name of pure punishment (or desert), will undermine even today's pathetic programs and worsen already bad correctional conditions.

Today, no one accepts the eighteenth-century notion that the penitentiary is a microcosm of the godly moral order. But the abandonment of rehabilitation, depending on the form it takes, may symbolize a pessimism not only about individual offenders but about larger social policy. Such a pessimism would reflect the breakup of the shared moral universe which Ignatieff described. If this happens, a liberal "success" could give penal policy in the late twentieth century an even more unpleasant turn than it took in the late eighteenth. "As a hopeful allegory for class relations in general," Ignatieff writes, the penitentiary "proved capable of surviving the repeated frustrations of reality because it spoke to a heart-felt middle class desire for a social order based on deferential reconciliation."[9] Today, the risk exists that a liberal abandonment of the rehabilitative ideal will constitute a hopeless allegory of class relations in general. Especially when one considers the racial composition of the inmate population, this is a most troubling feature of current liberal attitudes.

The liberal insensitivity to these bleak alternative futures is shown in the moratorium's intransigence. It is worth repeating the risky nature of the gamble that if construction money is stopped fewer people will go to prison. This seems to us a high-stakes bet that no outsider has a right to impose on others. If the reformers lose the bet—if incarceration rates do not drop when construction money dries up—offenders will pay the cost in even worse conditions than now exist. Even for a more sensitive federal legislator who sees this trap, another appears. If the Congress gives construction money to states that now have overcrowded conditions, those states may simply build more prisons that will soon be similarly overcrowded. If Congress refuses construction money to states that have overcrowded conditions, the current generation of inmates will certainly suffer, with future generations probably suffering as well.

Political Symbols and the Construction Debate

We have stressed the need for reform proposals, ours and those of others, to meet two quite different kinds of requirement. First, they must appear to "work" according to some rational standard of effectiveness. Second, they must respond to, or at least not offend, some unstated and perhaps even irrational expectations about what they "mean." This can be summarized in an analogy between two apparently unrelated construction debates in American public policy: whether to build a new generation of prisons and whether to build a new generation of strategic weapons. Sometimes one issue can be clarified by reference to another, especially if the debates are structurally similar. We think this is true here.

Over the past twenty years, there has been a running intellectual battle in strategic policy between friends and enemies of major capital investments in new weapons systems. With rare exceptions, members of the probuilding school have supported every major system proposed to Congress by the military establishment: Minuteman, Polaris, Poseidon, B-70, Dyna-Soar, MIRV, B-1, Trident, Cruise Missile, and most recently MX. With very high correlation, an analyst who supported any one of these systems is likely to have supported all the others. The same consistency is found among the antibuilders. Yet given the wide differences in the weapons systems' characteristics, the altered strategic balance at the time each was suggested, and the varying temperature of the international climate, these systems had wide variations in merit. It seems fair to say that something other than intrinsic merit played a part in the uniformity of responses on either side.

We suggest that the "something else" concerns the symbolic importance not only of the systems themselves but also of the decision to build or not to build them. To the probuilders, an affirmative decision on any and all systems symbolizes the government's commitment to protect the American people, to stand up to the Russians, to defend the American way of life. On the other side, the antibuilders see a decision not to build as symbolic of a recognition of the necessity of nonviolent solutions to international conflicts, and of a commitment not only to a more profound protection of the American people but to the protection of mankind.

Without being facetious, we see the strategic debate as a kind of intellectual and political game of capture-the-flag. From this perspective, it seems that the battle is fought not so much over the merits of a particular weapon, or over specific bureaucratic interests (though those play a part), but rather over legitimacy for a certain set of political values—for a particular definition of the general goal of protecting the American people.

The antibuilders in the strategic debate have often shown a relative inattention to and lack of expertise in the detailed characteristics of the systems under debate. This can be explained partly by their use of debating tactics; they do not want to grant the premises that would lead them into debate over the details of a system which they already know they oppose. But their willful inattention to operational details often weakens their case in the eyes of outside observers and reinforces the view that they are reflexively opposing defense rather than assessing whether the system will do what its proponents claim for it.

For over a decade the antibuilders won the debate hands down. From the early 1960s to the late 1970s few major new strategic systems were built and few were strongly recommended by the president to Congress. As a result, especially when aggravated by the deteriorating international climate of the past few years, a great deal of dissatisfaction accumulated among probuilders who lost in decision after decision. Apart from the ubiquitous concerns of agency and partisan politics, two more specific features of this dissatisfaction can be seen. One is a feeling that the dominant antibuilders (partly through their willful inattention to operational detail) had allowed existing strategic forces to degrade well beyond what would have happened merely through the passage of time. Another, more important feature is that the antibuilders had stopped doing analysis and had become fixated on holding down the size and even the complexity of the force. The probuilders felt that, in addition to losing a series of individual decisions, their general concerns and fundamental values were no longer taken seriously. Of course, the idea of protecting the American people was something they believed they understood better than did the antibuilders. But they believed also that antibuilders had stopped thinking carefully about the issues, and probuilders saw that as positively dangerous.

This explains their outrage at the antibuilders' initial refusal even to consider the possible weakness of the strategic triad after the Soviet deployments of the early 1970s. And it also explains why, once back in power, probuilders have shown a burst of enthusiasm for systems such as MX, which have obvious drawbacks but have come to symbolize their commitment to strategic forces. The antibuilders behaved as if once they won the debate in the 1960s they had won it for all time. They denied not only victory for specific probuilder programs but also denied legitimacy to their values. They forgot that in such battles the losing side does not give up its flag but rather sees itself as the loyal opposition with a competing and perfectly legitimate view of the national interest. The antibuilders' victory of the 1960s may even be regarded in the long run as Pyrrhic; their handling of it virtually guaranteed that a reflexive building program, with major long-term consequences, would begin as soon as the probuilders came back into positions of power.

The parallels with the prison construction debate are striking.

The generally polarized character is found here as well; nationally recognized experts can be found opposing not only specific construction programs in states widely separated by distance, conditions, and time, but also opposing all construction anywhere. This view is more extreme than anything in the strategic debate, although it may simply be that the prison moratorium people are less circumspect than their arms control counterparts.

A second similarity is in the historical and political development of the debate over the past fifteen or twenty years. As in defense, the correctional antibuilders dominated the scene both in theory and practice during the 1960s and early 1970s. The most prestigious thinking on the subject, epitomized by the Presidential Commissions of 1967 and 1973, either implicitly or explicitly opposed major building programs. The second panel endorsed a moratorium. In practice, the rate of prison construction dropped from earlier levels.

A third parallel is in the treatment by the dominant antibuilders of the forces that were in political decline. The probuilders were portrayed as opponents of civil liberties who wanted to throw the key away on hundreds of thousands of offenders for no better purpose than vengeance. Those who had defended the retributivist school of punishment, which after all had a long and respectable history in this and other cultures, were seen as reverting to an age of barbarism. In place of incarceration, the antibuilders offered the solution of community corrections, whereby all but the most serious offenders would be reintegrated into some (it turned out, mythical) community and live a law-abiding life. Having captured the policymaking and intellectual turf for a while, the antibuilders refused to acknowledge the legitimacy of the competing flag. As in the strategic debate, the competing flag had not been surrendered; yet its view of a different fundamental purpose for the criminal law was not only ignored, it was ridiculed.

The antibuilders' success, or at least their handling of it, may have been as Pyrrhic as the 1960s victory of the arms controllers. Antibuilders slighted both the deep retributivist tradition of the criminal sanction and the American single-minded equation of punishment with incarceration. They did not see that as long as most citizens believe that a convicted criminal gets off scot-free unless he is locked up at least for some period, there is not really any hope for reforms that offer only community corrections and probation as alternatives to the builders' policies. It is not surprising that there is a great deal of unused community corrections space at a time when the prisons and jails are bulging.

The final parallel is that, when the probuilders returned to political and intellectual power, many have used prison crowding

and judicial intervention to justify what we have criticized: a pan-
icked, reflexive, national-level, crisis-oriented response to prison
construction. Some appealed to the federal government to support
state and local programs, threatened a new wave of riots unless
new capacity was built, and supported construction wherever it
was proposed—irrespective of individual state problems, projected
populations, crime rates, or anything else.

The lessons of the analogy are clear, once it is recognized that
the debates have as much to do with political symbols as with
empirical data. (1) The outcome of these debates will not be
determined primarily by empirical data on missile performance
or recidivism rates or incarcerated population growth rates. (2)
Each side may manipulate such data to its own advantage, but the
important warning to observers is not to decry and dismiss those
manipulations. They should be seen as what they are—expressions
of deep and legitimate political ideas and aspirations. (3) We have
sought a long-term policy that will survive the volatile fashions in
articles about sentencing, as well as fluctuations in the prison
population. We have argued for the legitimacy of both sides' values
and tried to integrate them into a single, principled stance. This is a
tall order, but it seems literally a shame not to try.

Notes

Chapter 1

1. Totals drawn from U.S. Department of Justice, Law Enforcement Assistance Administration, National Criminal Justice Information and Statistics Service, *Sourcebook of Criminal Justice Statistics*, vols. for 1975 through 1979 (Washington, D.C.: Government Printing Office).

2. Abt Associates, "American Prisons and Jails," vol. 3, "Conditions and Costs of Confinement," chap. 6, 1979 draft, unpublished.

3. Coopers and Lybrand, *The Cost of Incarceration in New York City* (Hackensack, N.J.: National Council on Crime and Delinquency, 1978), cited in Marvin Adelson, "Correcting the Future," in National Institute of Law Enforcement, *Future of Corrections* (Washington, D.C.: Government Printing Office, 1978), p. 27.

4. National Commission on Law Observance and Enforcement (Wickersham Commission), *Report on Penal Institutions, Probation and Parole*, vol. 9 (Washington, D.C.: Government Printing Office, 1931).

5. Attica Commission, *Attica: The Official Report of the New York State Special Commission on Attica* (New York: Bantam Books, 1973).

6. For some illustrations of median time served to first release, see Abt Associates, *Prison Population and Policy Choices*, vol. 1, *Preliminary Report to Congress* (Washington, D.C.: Law Enforcement Assistance Administration, 1977), p. 165; cf. U.S. Department of Justice, *National Prisoner Statistics Special Report* (December 1976). The Abt final report notes that case studies of Florida and New York failed to find longer time served during the period of rising prison populations. See Abt Associates, *American Prisons and Jails*, vol. 2, *Population Trends and Projections* (Washington, D.C.: National Institute of Justice, 1980), p. 58.

7. U.S., Congress, Senate, *Congressional Record*, "LEAA and Prison Overcrowding," by Strom Thurmond, 10 August 1978, p. S.13097.

8. *U.S. News and World Report*, cited at ibid.

9. U.S., Congress, Senate, *Congressional Record*, "Statements on Introduced Bills and Joint Resolutions," by Joseph Biden, 27 July 1978, p. S.11972.

10. American Correctional Association, "Overcrowding in Prisons May Hold Seeds of Future Atticas," in Law Enforcement Assistance Administration *Newsletter* vol. 7, no. 10, p. 2.

11. *Corrections Digest* (Annandale, Va.), 11 August 1980, p. 1.

12. *New York Times*, 15 February 1980, p. 1.

13. U.S., Congress, Senate, *Congressional Record*, "Criminal Justice Construction Reform Act," 21 January 1981, pp. 1–8.

14. Frank Kermode, review of *The Culture of Narcissism* by Christopher Lasch, *New York Times Book Review*, 14 January 1979, p. 1.

15. U.S., Department of Justice, *Memorandum to Task Force Members: Status of Federal Corrections Policy Development*, 12 December 1977, p. 1.

16. T. D. Allman, "The Urban Crisis Leaves Town," *Harper's* (December 1978), p. 50.

17. Banning v. Looney, 213 F.2d 771 (10th Cir.), cert. denied, 348 U.S. 859 (1954).

18. For an excellent survey of this development, see James B. Jacobs, "The Prisoners' Rights Movement and Its Impacts," in Norval Morris and Michael Tonry, eds., *Crime and Justice: An Annual Review of Research*, vol. 2 (Chicago: University of Chicago Press, 1980).

19. Personal communication to the authors from Norman Carlson, 1979.

20. Phillip Johnson and Sheldon Messinger, "California's Determinate Sentencing Statute: History and Issues," mimeographed (1977), p. 2.

21. Abt Associates, *Prison Population and Policy Choices* (see n. 6 above), pp. 7–8.

22. The dubious media link of crowding with riots—although in fact riots were not unusually frequent during this period—increased interest even further.

23. David J. Rothman, *The Discovery of the Asylum* (Boston: Little, Brown & Co., 1971), p. 82.

24. Ibid., p. 88.

25. W. David Lewis, *From Newgate to Dannemora: The Rise of the Penitentiary in New York, 1796–1848* (Ithaca, N.Y.: Cornell University Press, 1965), p. viii.

26. William G. Nagel, *An American Archipelago . . . : The United States Bureau of Prisons* (Philadelphia: American Foundation Inc., Institute of Corrections, 1974), p. 4.

27. John P. Conrad, "Which Way to the Revolution?" in Matthew Matlin, ed., *Should We Build More Prisons?* (Hackensack, N.J.: National Council on Crime and Delinquency, 1977), pp. 6, 7, 12.

28. Rupert Cross, *Punishment, Prison and the Public* (London: Stevens & Sons, 1971), p. 142.

29. President's Commission on Law Enforcement and Administration of Justice, *Task Force Report: Corrections* (Washington: Government Printing Office, 1967), p. 45.

30. Abt Associates, *Prison Population and Policy Choices*, pp. 7–8.

31. American Friends Service Committee, *Struggle for Justice* (New York: Hill & Wang, 1971), p. 172.

32. National Council on Crime and Delinquency, "Institutional Construction: A Policy Statement," *Crime and Delinquency* 18 (1972): 331.

33. *Prisoners in America*, Report of the Forty-second American Assembly, 17–20 December 1972 (New York: American Assembly, Columbia University, 1973), p. 6.

34. National Advisory Commission on Criminal Justice Standards and Goals, *Task Force on Corrections* (Washington, D.C.: Government Printing Office, 1973), pp. 352, 357.

35. National Moratorium on Prison Construction, *The Moratorium on Prison Construction: Some Questions and Answers* (Boston: Unitarian Universalist Service Committee, 1978); see also William G. Nagel, "On Behalf of

a Moratorium on Prison Construction," *Crime and Delinquency* 23, no. 2 (April 1977): 154–72.

36. Milton G. Rector, "Are More Prisons Needed Now?" in Matthew Matlin, ed., *Should We Build More Prisons?* (Hackensack, N.J.: National Council on Crime and Delinquency, 1977), pp. 17–18.

37. U.S., Congress, Senate, Committee Report on the Departments of State, Justice, and Commerce, the Judiciary, and Related Agencies Appropriations Bill, 1977 (Report 94-964 in *Senate Reports*, 94th Cong., 1976), pp. 22–23.

38. Eugene Doleschal, "Rate and Length of Imprisonment: How Does the United States Compare with The Netherlands, Denmark and Sweden?" *Crime and Delinquency* 23 (1977): 52.

39. William G. Nagel, *The New Red Barn: A Critical Look at the Modern American Prison* (New York: Walker & Co., 1973), p. 10.

40. U.S., Congress, House Committee on the Judiciary, Hearings, *Prison Construction Plans and Policy*, 94th Cong., 1975, p. 104.

41. C. Northcote Parkinson, *Parkinson's Law* (Cambridge, Mass.: Houghton Mifflin Co., 1957), p. 2.

42. National Council on Crime and Delinquency, p. 332.

43. Rector, p. 20.

44. U.S., Congress, House Committee on the Judiciary, Hearings, pp. 11, 19.

45. Aaron Wildavsky, "Doing Better and Feeling Worse: The Political Pathology of Health Policy," *Daedalus* (Winter 1977), pp. 105–24.

46. U.S., Congress, House Committee on the Judiciary, Hearings, p. 4.

47. U.S. Advisory Commission on Intergovernmental Relations, *State-Local Relations in the Criminal Justice System* (Washington: Government Printing Office, 1971), p. 54.

48. National Council on Crime and Delinquency, "The Nondangerous Offender Should Not Be Imprisoned: A Policy Statement," *Crime and Delinquency* 19, no. 4 (1973): 449, 456.

49. National Council on Crime and Delinquency, "Institutional Construction," p. 332.

50. Ibid.

51. Conrad, "Which Way to the Revolution?" pp. 10, 14.

52. Marvin E. Frankel, *Criminal Sentences: Law without Order* (New York: Hill & Wang, 1973), pp. 5, 7.

53. Erik Olin Wright, ed., *The Politics of Punishment: A Critical Analysis of Prisons in America* (New York: Harper & Row, 1973), p. 33.

54. U.S., Congress, House Committee on the Judiciary, Hearings, p. 40.

55. Conrad, "Which Way to the Revolution?" pp. 6, 10, 11.

56. Conrad, "Response to Milton G. Rector," in Matlin, p. 28 (see n. 27 above).

57. Conrad, "Which Way to the Revolution?" pp. 10, 11.

58. James Q. Wilson, cited in Rob Wilson, "U.S. Prison Population Again Hits New High," *Corrections Magazine* 3, no. 1 (1977): 22.

59. James Q. Wilson, "The Political Feasibility of Punishment," in J. B. Cederblom and William L. Blizek, eds., *Justice and Punishment* (Cambridge, Mass.: Ballinger Publishing Co., 1977), pp. 109–23.

60. Gresham M. Sykes, *Crime and Society* (New York: Random House, 1958), p. 81.

61. Wilson, cited in Rob Wilson, p. 22.

62. Conrad, "Which Way to the Revolution?" p. 30.

63. Ibid., pp. 10, 11.

64. Rector, p. 18.

65. Robert Martinson, quoted in Michael S. Serrill, "Critics of Corrections Speak Out," *Corrections Magazine 2*, no. 3 (1976): 26.

66. Conrad, "Which Way to the Revolution?" p. 12.

67. Wilson, "The Political Feasibility of Punishment," p. 120.

68. Franklin E. Zimring, "Making the Punishment Fit the Crime: A Consumer's Guide to Sentencing Reform," University of Chicago Law School, Occasional Paper no. 12, 1977, p. 13.

69. Wilson, "The Political Feasibility of Punishment," p. 120.

70. Rector, "Response to John P. Conrad," in Matlin, p. 33 (see n. 36 above).

71. American Correctional Association.

72. Dick Howard and Michael Kannensohn, *A State-supported Local Correctional System: The Minnesota Experience* (Lexington, Ky.: Council of State Governments, 1977), passim.

73. Abt Associates, *Prison Population and Policy Choices* (see n. 6 above), p. 1.

74. National Advisory Commission (see n. 34 above), p. 1.

Chapter 2

1. President's Commission on Law Enforcement and Administration of Justice, *Task Force Report: Corrections* (Washington, D.C.: Government Printing Office, 1967), p. 45.

2. National Advisory Commission on Criminal Justice Standards and Goals, *Task Force Report on Corrections* (Washington, D.C.: Government Printing Office, 1973), pp. 358, 397.

3. James Q. Wilson, "The Political Feasibility of Punishment," in J. B. Cederblom and W. L. Blizek, eds., *Justice and Punishment* (Cambridge, Mass.: Ballinger Publishing Co., 1977).

4. See U.S. Department of Justice, Law Enforcement Assistance Administration, *Sourcebook of Criminal Justice Statistics 1973* (1973), sec. 6, and *Sourcebook of Criminal Justice Statistics 1978* (1979), sec. 6.

5. National Commission on Law Observance and Enforcement (Wickersham Commission), *Report on Penal Institutions, Probation and Parole*, vol. 9 (Montclair, N.J.: Patterson Smith, 1968), p. 170.

6. Ibid., p. 11.

7. Frederick E. Haynes, *The American Prison System* (New York: McGraw-Hill Book Co., 1939), p. 265.

8. Orlando F. Lewis, *The Development of American Prisons and Prison Customs, 1776–1845* (1922; reprint ed., Montclair, N.J.: Patterson Smith, 1967), p. 111.

9. Ibid., pp. 111–12.

10. Great Britain, *Parliamentary Papers*, vol. 46 (*Crime and Punishment, Prisons*, vol. 2, August 1834), "Report of William Crawford, Esq. on the Penitentiaries of the United States, addressed to His Majesty's Principal Secretary of State for the Home Department," pp. 19–20.

11. Ibid.

12. Dorothea L. Dix, *Remarks on Prisons and Prison Discipline in the*

United States, 2d ed. (Philadelphia: Joseph Kite & Co., 1845), p. 45.

13. Harry E. Barnes and Negley K. Teeters, *New Horizons in Criminology: The American Crime Problem,* 2d ed. (New York: Prentice-Hall, Inc., 1951), p. 488.

14. U.S., Congress, House Committee on the Judiciary, Subcommittee on Courts, Civil Liberties, and the Administration of Justice, *Prison Plans and Policy: Hearings before a Subcommittee of the Committee on the Judiciary,* 94th Cong., 1st sess., 28–29 July 1975, p. 7.

15. James B. Jacobs, *Stateville, The Penitentiary in Mass Society* (Chicago, Ill.: University of Chicago Press, 1977).

16. Rated capacities can also be circumvented in a different direction. In 1977, for example, California's Department of Corrections proposal to the California State Joint Legislative Budget Committee computed occupancy level on the basis of "active beds." The number of active beds was determined by subtracting the number of beds "deactivated" because of declining inmate populations from the design capacity. By this ingenious method of calculation, the occupancy level for December 31, 1976, for male active beds was 92 percent and for female beds 88 percent, whereas the figures, using design capacity, would have been 85 percent and 77 percent, respectively.

17. John Howard, *The State of the Prisons* (1777; reprint ed., New York: E. P. Dutton & Co., 1929), p. 105.

18. Sidney and Beatrice Webb, *English Prisons Under Local Government* (1922; reprint ed., Hamden, Conn.: Archon Books, 1963), p. 119.

19. 471 Fed. Supp. 1095 (SDNY 1978).

20. 47 U.S.L.W. 4507 (U.S. Supreme Court, 1979).

21. National Advisory Commission, p. 358.

22. See Commission on Accreditation for Corrections, *Manual of Standards for Adult Correctional Institutions* (Rockville, Md.: American Correctional Association, 1977), p. 27; U.S. Department of Justice, "Federal Standards for Corrections" (June 1978 draft), p. 10; Abt Associates, *Prison Population and Policy Choices,* vol. 1, *Preliminary Report to Congress* (Washington, D.C.: Law Enforcement Assistance Administration, 1977), p. 11; National Sheriffs' Association, *A Handbook on Jail Architecture* (Washington, D.C.: National Sheriffs' Association, 1975), p. 63; United Nations, First U.N. Congress on the Prevention of Crime and the Treatment of Offenders, Geneva, *Standard Minimum Rules for the Treatment of Prisoners,* 1956, p. 11.

23. Philadelphia Society for Alleviating the Miseries of Public Prisons, *Extracts and Remarks on the Subjects of Punishment and Reformation of Criminals* (Philadelphia: Z. Poulson, 1790), p. 19.

24. National Commission on Law Observance and Enforcement (Wickersham Commission), p. 11; and U.S. Department of Commerce, Bureau of the Census, *Prisoners in State and Federal Prisons and Reformatories, 1927* (Washington, D.C.: Government Printing Office, 1931), p. 8.

25. William G. Nagel, "On Behalf of a Moratorium on Prison Construction," *Crime and Delinquency* 23, no. 2 (April 1977): 154–72.

26. Kenneth Carlson, *American Prisons and Jails,* vol. 2. *Population Trends and Projections* (Cambridge, Mass.: Abt Associates Inc., 1980), 53–56.

27. In fact, statistical claims about individual states are generally insupportable because the effects of the small number of prison openings in

any given state are easily obscured by the mass of independent random and systematic sources of change in prison populations.

Chapter 3

1. See Georg Rusche and Otto Kirchheimer, *Punishment and Social Structure* (New York: Columbia University Press, 1939), where the authors refer to "the illusion that a specific penal practice is bound up with a specific penal theory" (p. 141) and state that "we are actually turning things upside down... if we take at its face value the imaginary power of doctrine over reality, instead of understanding the theoretical innovation as the expression of a necessary or already accomplished change in social praxis" (p. 142). In their view, "the use or avoidance of specific punishments, and the intensity of penal practices... are determined by social forces, above all by economic and then fiscal forces" (p. 5).

2. Great Britain, Parliament, House of Commons, *The Reduction of Pressure on the Prison System*, Fifteenth Report from the Expenditure Committee, vol. 1 (1978), pp. xvi–xvii.

3. The Right Honorable Roy Jenkins M.P., Principal Secretary of State for the Home Department, "Address to the National Association for the Care and Resettlement of Offenders (NACRO) Annual General Meeting," 21 July 1975.

4. *Times* (London), 1 May 1980, "More a Hope Than a Policy," p. 17.

5. *Times* (London), 1 May 1980, Robert Kilroy-Silk, M.P., see report "Mr. Whitelaw 'has missed the real issue of numbers.'"

6. Blake McKelvey, *American Prisons* (Montclair, N.J.: Patterson Smith, 1977), p. 7.

7. Ibid., p. 8.

8. Ibid., p. 9.

9. Orlando F. Lewis, *The Development of American Prisons and Prison Customs, 1776–1845* (1922; reprint ed., Montclair, N.J.: Patterson Smith, 1967), p. 25.

10. McKelvey (1968 ed.), p. 7.

11. Ibid., p. 172.

12. Ibid., p. 32.

13. Ibid., p. 76.

14. Ibid., p. 154.

15. William Blackstone, *Commentaries on the Laws of England* (London: W. Walker, 1826), pp. 311–12.

16. Sidney and Beatrice Webb, *English Prisons Under Local Government* (1922; reprint ed., Hamden, Conn.: Archon Books, 1963), p. 47.

17. George Ives, *A History of Penal Methods* (London: Stanley Paul & Co., 1914), p. 177.

18. Ibid., p. 179.

19. Webb, pp. 48–49.

20. A. G. L. Shaw, *Convicts and the Colonies* (London: Faber & Faber, 1966), p. 21.

21. Quoted in ibid., p. 32.

22. Frederick H. Wines, *Punishment and Reformation* (New York: Thomas Y. Crowell Co., 1910), p. 183.

23. Max Grunhut, *Penal Reform* (Oxford: Clarendon Press, 1948), p. 73.

24. Hans von Hentig, *Punishment: The Origin, Purpose and Psychology* (London: William Hodge & Co., 1937), pp. 18–19.

25. Sir Lionel Fox, *The English Prison and Borstal Systems* (London: Routledge & Kegan Paul, 1952), p. 31.

26. Jeremy Bentham, *Principles of Penal Law*, in J. Bowring, ed., *Works*, vol. 1, bk. 5 (London: Simpkin, Marshall & Co., 1843), p. 497.

27. Michael Ignatieff, *A Just Measure of Pain* (New York: Pantheon Books, 1978), p. 67.

28. Quoted in ibid., p. 68.

29. Ibid., p. 58.

30. Gladstone Committee, quoted in Ives, p. 202.

31. Sir Edmund du Cane, *An Account of the Manner in Which Sentences of Penal Servitude Are Carried Out in England* (London: Millbank Prison, 1882), p. 10.

32. Fox, p. 51.

33. Ibid.

34. Sir Edmund du Cane, *The Punishment and Prevention of Crime* (London: Macmillan & Co., 1885), p. 109.

35. Great Britain, Home Department, *Report of the Departmental Committee on Prisons (The Gladstone Report)*, cmd. 7702 (1895), para. 15.

36. Quoted in Gordon Rose, *The Struggle for Penal Reform* (Chicago: Quadrangle Books, 1961), p. 39.

37. Sir Evelyn Ruggles-Brise, *The English Prison System* (London: Macmillan & Co., 1921), p. 75.

38. Fox, p. 16.

39. House Lords Committee, quoted in Fox, p. 2.

40. du Cane, *An Account of the Manner*, p. 10.

41. Ruggles-Brise, p. 40.

42. Sir Godfrey Lushington, quoted in *The Gladstone Report* (see n. 35 above), para. 11, p. 496.

43. Ibid., para. 11, p. 480.

44. Rusche and Kirchheimer, p. 140.

45. Webb, p. 202.

46. Fox, p. 65.

47. Quoted in Shane Leslie, *Sir Evelyn Ruggles-Brise* (London: John Murray, 1938), p. 103.

48. Quoted in Webb, p. vii.

49. Ibid., p. 248.

50. Great Britain, Home Department, *Report of the Commissioners of Prisoners and Directors of Convict Prisons*, cmd. 1761 (1922), p. 22.

52. David J. Rothman, *Conscience and Convenience* (Boston: Little, Brown & Co., 1980), p. 29.

53. Ibid., p. 31.

54. Ibid.

55. Leslie, p. 100.

56. Ruggles-Brise, p. ix.

57. Edwin H. Sutherland, "The Decreasing Prison Population of England," *Journal of Criminal Law and Criminology* 24 (1934): 880.

58. Thomas Mott Osborne, *Society and Prisons* (New Haven, Conn.: Yale University Press, 1924), p. 216.

59. Thomas Mott Osborne, *Prisons and Common Sense* (Philadelphia: J. B. Lippincott Co., 1924), p. 10.

60. Roscoe Pound, *Criminal Justice in America* (1923).

61. Claude Mullins, *Fifteen Years' Hard Labour* (London: Victor Collancz Ltd., 1949), p. 100.

62. Ruggles-Brise, p. 90.

63. Rupert Cross, *Punishment, Prison and the Public* (London: Stevens & Sons, 1971), pp. 101, 98–99.

64. Fox, p. 128.

65. Ibid., pp. 113–14.

66. Great Britain, Home Office, *The Length of Prison Sentences, Interim Report of the Advisory Council on the Penal System* (London: Her Majesty's Stationary Office, 1977), pp. 2–3.

67. Great Britain, Home Office, *A Review of Criminal Justice Policy 1976*, Home Office Working Paper (London: Her Majesty's Stationary Office, 1977), pp. 48–49.

68. Rusche and Kirchheimer, p. 142.

69. Mary Peter Mack, *A Bentham Reader* (New York: Western Publishing Co., 1969), p. 192.

Chapter 4

1. Newman v. Alabama, 559 F.2d 283, 291 (5th Cir.), (1977).

2. The paraphrase is from John Leonard reviewing Hobsbawm in the *New York Times*, 9 April 1981, p. C23.

3. Henry M. Hart, "The Aims of the Criminal Law," *Law and Contemporary Problems* 23 (1958): 402.

4. Quoted in American Friends Service Committee, *Struggle for Justice* (New York: Hill & Wang, 1971), p. 21.

5. Ernest van den Haag, *Punishing Criminals* (New York: Basic Books, 1975), p. 21.

6. Quoted in Michael Ignatieff, *A Just Measure of Pain* (New York: Pantheon Books, 1978), p. 75.

7. Harry E. Barnes, *The Evolution of Penology in Pennsylvania* (Montclair, N.J.: Patterson Smith, 1968), p. 30.

8. David J. Rothman, *The Discovery of the Asylum* (Boston: Little, Brown & Co., 1971), p. 29.

9. Ibid., p. 45.

10. Quoted in ibid, p. 27.

11. Ibid., p. 53.

12. Ibid.

13. Ibid., p. 52.

14. Blake McKelvey, *American Prisons* (Montclair, N.J.: Patterson Smith, 1977), p. 3.

15. Graeme Newman, *The Punishment Response* (Philadelphia: J. B. Lippincott Co., 1978), p. 187.

16. Rothman, *The Discovery of the Asylum*, p. 39.

17. Ignatieff, p. 74.

18. Quoted in ibid.

19. Paul W. Tappan, *Crime, Justice and Correction* (New York: McGraw-Hill Book Co., 1960), p. 601.

20. Rothman, *The Discovery of the Asylum*, p. 61.

21. Cesare Beccaria, *On Crimes and Punishments*, trans. Henry Paolucci (Indianapolis: Bobbs-Merrill Co., 1963), pp. 43–44.

22. Caleb Lownes, "An Account of the Gaol and Penitentiary House of Philadelphia, and of the Interior Mangement Thereof," in William Bradford, *An Enquiry How Far the Punishment of Death is Necessary in Pennsylvania* (Philadelphia: T. Dobson, 1793; reprint ed. for J. Johnson, 1795), p. 101.

23. Quoted in W. David Lewis, *From Newgate to Dannemora: The Rise of the Penitentiary in New York, 1796–1848* (Ithaca, N.Y.: Cornell University Press, 1965), pp. 29–30.

24. Ibid., p. 32.

25. Orlando F. Lewis, *The Development of American Prisons and Prison Customs, 1776–1845* (1922; reprint ed., Montclair, N.J.: Patterson Smith, 1967), p. 26.

26. Quoted in W. David Lewis, p. 43.

27. Quoted in ibid., p. 50.

28. Quoted in ibid., p. 63.

29. Ibid., p. 87.

30. Quoted in ibid., p. 89.

31. Ibid., p. 92.

32. Ibid., p. 56.

33. Ibid., p. 56.

34. Rothman, *The Discovery of the Asylum*, pp. 62, 88.

35. Gustave de Beaumont and Alexis de Tocqueville, *On the Penitentiary System in the United States and Its Application in France*, trans. Francis Lieber (Carbondale: Southern Illinois University Press, 1964), p. 208, n. 4.

36. Quoted in George Wilson Pierson, *Tocqueville and Beaumont in America* (New York: Oxford University Press, 1938), p. 133.

37. Quoted in ibid., p. 473.

38. Ibid., p. 119.

39. Beaumont and Tocqueville, p. 80.

40. Ibid., p. 90.

41. Ibid., p. 89.

42. Pierson, p. 88.

43. Beaumont and Tocqueville, p. 82.

44. Quoted in McKelvey, p. 86.

45. Ibid.

46. Roscoe Pound, "The Causes of Popular Dissatisfaction with the Administration of Justice," *ABA Reports* 29 (1906): 395.

47. David J. Rothman, *Conscience and Convenience* (Boston: Little, Brown & Co., 1980), passim.

48. Beaumont and Tocqueville, p. 38.

49. Norval Morris, *The Future of Imprisonment* (Chicago: University of Chicago Press, 1974).

50. Beaumont and Tocqueville, p. 26.

51. David J. Rothman, "Decarcerating Prisoners and Patients," *Civil Liberties Review* 1 (1973): 24.

52. David E. Greenberg, "Rehabilitation Is Still Punishment," in William Adler-Geller, "The Problem of Prisons: A Way Out?" *Humanist* (May–June 1972), p. 28.

53. William G. Nagel, *An American Archipelago . . . : The United States Bureau of Prisons* (Philadelphia: American Foundation Inc., Institute of Corrections, 1974).

54. James Q. Wilson, cited in Rob Wilson, "U.S. Prison Population Again Hits New High," *Corrections Magazine* 3, no. 1 (1977): 22.

55. Personal communication to the authors from Herman Kahn.

56. American Friends Service Committee (see n. 4 above), p. 24.

57. Glanville Williams, *Salmond on Jurisprudence*, 11th ed. (London: Sweet & Maxwell, 1957), p. 121.

58. National Advisory Commission on Criminal Justice Standards and

Goals, *Task Force Report on Corrections* (Washington, D.C.: Government Printing Office, 1973), p. 1.

59. Alfred Blumstein, Jacqueline Cohen, and Daniel Nagin, eds., *Deterrence and Incapacitation: Estimating the Effects of Criminal Sanctions on Crime Rates* (Washington, D.C.: National Academy of Sciences, 1978), p. 7.

60. Johan Thorsten Sellin, *The Death Penalty: A Report for the Model Penal Code Project of the American Law Institute* (Philadelphia: American Law Institute, 1959).

61. Isaac Ehrlich, "The Deterrent Effect of Capital Punishment: A Question of Life and Death," *American Economic Review* 65 (1975): 397.

62. Franklin E. Zimring and Gordon Hawkins, *Deterrence: The Legal Threat in Crime Control* (Chicago: University of Chicago Press, 1973), pp. 254–55, 263–65, 288–90.

63. National Advisory Commission, p. 1.

64. Stephan Van Dine et al., "The Incapacitation of the Dangerous Offender: A Statistical Experiment," *Journal of Research in Crime and Delinquency* 14 (January 1977): 23–24, and "Response to Our Critics," ibid., 15 (January 1978): 135–39; Reuel and Shlomo Shinnar, "The Effects of the Criminal Justice System on the Control of Crime," *Law and Society Review* 9 (Summer 1975): 581–612; Joan Petersilia and Peter W. Greenwood, "Mandatory Prison Sentences: Their Projected Effects on Crime and Prison Populations," *Journal of Criminal Law and Criminology* 69, no. 4 (1978): 604–15.

65. National Council on Crime and Delinquency, "The Nondangerous Offender Should Not Be Imprisoned: A Policy Statement," *Crime and Delinquency* 19, no. 4 (1973): 449.

66. National Council on Crime and Delinquency, Model Sentencing Act, 2d ed. (Hackensack, N.J.: NCCD), p. 95.

67. Milton G. Rector, "Are More Prisons Needed Now?" in Matthew Matlin, ed., *Should We Build More Prisons?* (Hackensack, N.J.: National Council on Crime and Deinquency, 1977), p. 19.

68. Morris, p. 60.

69. Ibid., pp. 59–60.

70. Andrew von Hirsch, *Doing Justice: The Choice of Punishments*, Report of the Committee for the Study of Incarceration (New York: Hill & Wang, 1976), passim.

71. Andrew von Hirsch and Kathleen Hanrahan, *The Question of Parole* (Cambridge, Mass.: Ballinger Publishing Co., 1979), p. 30.

Chapter 5

1. William Eden (First Baron Auckland), *Principles of Penal Law*, 2d ed. (London: printed for B. White & T. Codell, 1771), p. 50.

2. Abt Associates, *Prison Population and Policy Choices*, vol. 1, *Preliminary Report to Congress* (Washington, D.C.: Law Enforcement Assistance Administration, 1977), p. 233; and Abt Associates, "Working Paper on Community-based Corrections" (n.d.).

3. Eugene Doleschal, "Rate and Length of Imprisonment: How Does the United States Compare with the Netherlands, Denmark and Sweden?" *Crime and Delinquency* 23 (1971): 52.

4. Abt Associates, *Prison Population and Policy Choices*, p. 165.

5. National Council on Crime and Delinquency, "The Nondangerous Offender Should Not Be Imprisoned: A Policy Statement," *Crime and Delinquency* 19, no. 4 (1973): 456.

6. Milton G. Rector, "Are More Prisons Needed Now?" in Matthew Matlin, ed., *Should We Build More Prisons?* (Hackensack, N.J.: National Council on Crime and Delinquency, 1977), p. 19.

7. James Q. Wilson, cited in Rob Wilson, "U.S. Prison Population Again Hits New High," *Corrections Magazine* 3, no. 1 (1977): 22.

8. Wendell Bell, "Bias, Probability and Prison Population: A New Setting for Affirmative Action," in National Institute of Law Enforcement, *Future of Corrections* (Washington, D.C.: Government Printing Office, 1978), p. 1.

9. David Greenberg and Drew Humphries, "The Co-optation of Fixed Sentencing Reform," *Crime and Delinquency* 26, no. 2 (1980): 206–25.

10. Macklin Fleming, *The Price of Perfect Justice* (New York: Basic Books, 1974).

11. American Law Institute, *Model Penal Code: Proposed Official Draft* (Philadelphia: American Law Institute, 1962), sec. 7.01; and Norval Morris, *The Future of Imprisonment* (Chicago: University of Chicago Press, 1974), p. 60.

12. Abt Associates, *Prison Population and Policy Choices,* p. 172.

13. As recently as three years ago, some observers argued that the Illinois prison population had stabilized at about 11,000. It has since substantially exceeded this level.

14. The analysis presented here was carried out with the assistance of Kenneth Carlson on the basis of unpublished data collected by Abt Associates for the federal survey. The final report was published as *American Prisons and Jails* (Washington, D.C.: National Institute of Justice, 1980).

15. Abt Associates, *Prison Population and Policy Choices,* p. 172.

16. Pugh v. Locke, 406 F. Supp. 318 (M.D. Ala. 1976), affirmed and remanded by the U.S. Court of Appeals for the Fifth Circuit, 16 September 1977, no. 76-2269; also, personal communication to authors from Alfred J. Blumstein.

17. Morris (see n. 11 above), pp. 20–22.

18. Norval Morris and Gordon Hawkins, *Letter to the President on Crime Control* (Chicago: University of Chicago Press, 1977), p. 67.

19. Morris, p. 26.

20. Francis A. Allen, *The Decline of the Rehabilitative Ideal* (New Haven, Conn.: Yale University Press, forthcoming).

21. Rector, "Response to John P. Conrad," in Matlin, p. 33 (see n. 6 above).

22. Reuel Shinnar and Shlomo Shinnar, "The Effects of the Criminal Justice System on the Control of Crime," *Law and Society Review* 9 (Summer 1975): 581, 605.

23. Joan Petersilia and Peter W. Greenwood, "Mandatory Prison Sentences: Their Projected Effects on Crime and Prison Populations," *Journal of Criminal Law and Criminology* 69, no. 4 (1978): 606, 607.

24. Ibid., pp. 607–8.

25. Ibid., pp. 610, 613.

26. Ibid., pp. 610, 614.

27. Norval Morris and Michael Tonry, "Black Crime, Black Victims," *Chicago Tribune,* 18–21 August 1980.

Chapter 6

1. George Ives, *A History of Penal Methods* (London: Stanley Paul & Co., 1914), p. 176.

2. Ibid., p. 321.

3. George Wilson Pierson, *Tocqueville and Beaumont in America* (New York: Oxford University Press, 1938), p. 700.

4. Ibid., p. 703.

5. Ibid., p. 702.

6. Michael Ignatieff, *A Just Measure of Pain* (New York: Pantheon Books, 1978), p. 216.

7. Ibid., p. 79.

8. Ibid., p. 73.

9. Ibid., p. 213.

Index